Behind every man there is a great woman. In my case, there happens to be four of them!

I send my love and thanks to my lovely wife, Mhairi, and to my three terrific daughters, Gilan, Mhairi and Marina.

They did not let me go.

Love also to my six grandchildren, Victoria, Fergus, Mhairi, Murdo, Ross and Cruz.

I also dedicate this book to the memory of the legendary Billy McNeill, the wonderful man who signed me for Celtic and understood why I had to leave him and go to Borussia Dortmund.

Billy signed me for Celtic and changed my life.

Thank you always, big man.

MURDO MACLEOD

Contents

Introduction

I WOULD NEVER WISH to have my life defined by illness or infirmity.

I might now have a disabled pass which I can put on the windscreen of my car for parking purposes but I still think I have an open road in front of me when it comes to negotiating the latter stages of my life. A life that I would rather be remembered for because of what I did on the football pitch while winning five league titles, two Scottish Cups and one League Cup with Celtic. A nine-year spell spent at one of the biggest football clubs in the world, and a time which earned me the right to join another institution within the game, Borussia Dortmund.

Germany gave me another cup win which I treasure and after that came a move back to Scotland with Hibs, where I helped the club win the League Cup at Hampden.

Along the way, there were twenty international caps for Scotland and my time working in the game was made exceptional by my final act as a coach. I was assistant to the late Wim Jansen when Celtic stopped Rangers from winning Ten in a Row with a title win of our own that was as dramatic as any moment I had known in my professional life. You can't really better a title win of your own after a decade of despair when it comes on the final day of the season in front of sixty thousand of your own fans, emotionally moved to the point of delirium, can you? Unbelievable scenes!

Why would I want any, or all, of that to be overshadowed by medical problems, no matter how severe, or even life threatening they might have been? Never at any stage in my life after football have I asked myself that self-pitying question, "Why me?" And there is one simple reason why I have never done that, even when life seemed to be ebbing away from me or when I have had to deal with the physical consequences of operations that have gone wrong. And that's because I think I have actually had a great life and I won't allow anything to detract from that now.

As well as a career in football that I wouldn't change for anything, I have a wonderful family and incredible friendships I have made with people from all over the world. And I've always lived my life in the best way I could and spent time with people who share a similar outlook, looking for the right sort of qualities in people, like honesty, which I believe is not only a virtue but a prerequisite in any decent human being.

I have been blessed by being able to do what I most wanted to do in life from the earliest days of my youth, and that was play football to the highest professional standard I could. I played the game, coached the game and became a radio and television pundit who talked about the game. What happened when the final whistle blew on that side of my life wasn't pleasant but I never hid away from it or felt self-conscious because my body had taken a pounding and I bore the physical scars of what I had been through.

I've spoken publicly about what has happened to me and I've gone out and appeared in front of people even when it was painful simply to stand up straight. And the reason I did all of that was quite simple, really – it's been for the people who have kept me going in recent years. I have got back from men and women in the street a warmth that has been gratifying in the extreme.

At Celtic and Dortmund, I played in front of people who were predominantly working class and that was the background I came from myself. You give something of yourself to those people and they give their affection back to you. It's something I hugely value and enjoy, something that really does mean a lot to me.

There will be plenty of references here to hospitals, operations, crutches, wheelchairs and zimmers. All of that is unavoidable because they were all part of the story that takes me to today.

There'll be stories of self-amputation, pain relief and physical impairment. Once again, those references can't be left out because all of it is true and any attempt to skip over the unpleasant bits would be a dishonest account of my life. None of us can airbrush the bits of our lives we'd rather not remember. What happened to me after the immersion in football stopped wasn't, and never will be, the whole story. I had a good career and I think my efforts were properly appreciated and respected wherever I worked.

But, in truth, there is an emptiness that comes after you stop playing the game, although I tried never to let that get the better of me. Instead, I took the view that I was lucky enough to have been involved in so many moments on the park that gave tens of thousands of people immense enjoyment. And I felt privileged to have had the time to do that and be properly recognised for it.

I don't have a fund of racy stories about ferocious rows with people I have come across in the game since I began playing for a living in the 1970s. You can't be in football for that length of time and never encounter people you could have done without, it would be deceitful to pretend otherwise, but they will be mentioned in passing as opposed to being used as a source of revenge for therapeutic purposes. Life has thrown enough at me without bothering to dwell on what is relatively unimportant by comparison.

There have been times when getting on with life has been easier said than done for me due to health issues, but my intention has always been to move on rather than wallow in self-pity. The mental strength I was fortunate enough to possess made me feel grateful that I still had a life to get on with, especially during those times when I was engaged in a fight with my own mortality.

There was a time when one hospital sent me home after a particularly painful procedure with a wheelchair to help me get around and spare my feet, which no longer had toes. But I took it back after a week because I was determined that I was literally going to stand on my own two feet, no matter what had happened to them. I refuse to be a victim. I demand the chance to start all over again and be my own man.

Sometimes I watch football matches on television and my mind drifts back to the way it used to be for me, but I don't live in the past. I have the here and now to contend with.

I have paid a physical price for surviving an operation that left me on a ventilator and introduced complications which have had serious repercussions. But I console myself with the thought that I was part of something at football clubs that meant so much to so many people. That is my legacy, not the paraphernalia of hospitals, clinics and doctors' surgeries.

I dreamed of having a big life in football and I got to live the dream. We all start off somewhere, but it's where we finish that's important.

1
The Gift of Life

LIFE IS A GIFT.

What you do with the gift depends on how hard you're willing to work.

Throughout my life I have seen everything in my way as a challenge to be confronted by applying professional discipline. I meet everything head on and with an absolute determination not to fail.

To this day I would want to beat my six grand-children if I was playing tiddlywinks with them, and they know that. It's an attitude of mind that sustained me throughout a football career which began at Dumbarton as a teenager and took me to Celtic, where I was part of a side which won five league titles, two Scottish Cups and a League Cup.

I was blessed to be the one who scored the goal that won the championship at the end of my first season at the club in the match immortalised as the '4–2 game' by those who were there and others who've been brought up on stories of that dramatic night against Rangers. And humbled when that goal was voted by the Celtic supporters as the greatest ever scored in an Old Firm derby.

Twenty-five years ago Wim Jansen and myself formed the management team that prevented Rangers from winning ten titles in a row at the end of a tumultuous season which will probably live forever in the minds of the Celtic supporters who went through every emotional episode with us over those memorable months.

Those were achievements I had a degree of control over because I could put in as much effort as was humanly possible in the interests of achieving a collective goal. But after my career was over there then came two moments of personal crisis over which I had absolutely no influence. It was, on two occasions spread over a twelve-year period, a time when I was forced to look over the edge and obliged to measure the distance between life and death. In those moments you have no control over what happens next and have to place your mortality in the hands of others, and they need to know that they have my deeply felt gratitude for now being able to tell the story.

It's a story I tell with a degree of reluctance because when footballers, or former players, find themselves in a situation like that, their lives tend to be hijacked and played out in the full glare of the public gaze. I had a wife, Mhairi, and three daughters, Gilan, Mhairi and Marina, to protect and they somehow managed to negotiate both those moments of sustained anxiety while being a source of unflinching support to me. They should know how thankful I am to have had them on my side.

The first issue came in 2010 when I had a heart operation which needed to be carried out under emergency conditions. I wouldn't have seen the following day if the surgeon who saved my life hadn't got me into the operating theatre in time.

The second flirtation with death came in 2022 when the heart valve that had been inserted in my original operation needed to be replaced. It had only been supposed to last a decade, but what I thought would be a fairly routine procedure turned into something much more problematic.

I am going to recount the story of what happened straight off the bat and get it out of the way simply to underline the fact that I am eternally grateful to everyone who did what they did to give me the gift of life. Every doctor, nurse and hospital porter should know I thank them for their dedication and diligence. Every friend and football supporter whose love and best wishes sustained me through the darkest of times gave me the strength which has allowed me to be here today.

But, after I have told this part of my story, I am going to park the subject and get on with talking about things like the Celtic fans recognising me with that chant of 'Murdo! Murdo!' which rang out during games when I was proud to wear the club's shirt. It was like a doorbell's chimes, and it meant so much to me that it is actually the sound you hear now when you ring the doorbell outside of my house!

The fans always had my back, and they had my sincere affection in return. I never, ever let a request for an autograph or a photograph go unanswered, no matter how long it took me to get away from Celtic Park after training or matches. They took me to their hearts, and I appreciated their warmth and concern when it was my heart that became the problem.

I was working for BBC Radio Scotland at Firhill, the home of Partick Thistle and a club I would eventually go on to manage, one Saturday afternoon in 2010 when I started to exhibit the symptoms which led to my first confrontation with my own mortality. I had developed a rasping and uncontrollable cough but I had no idea it would ultimately lead to an ambulance with its blue light on transferring me from one hospital to another that was better equipped to deal with a man who was slipping away from this world to another.

There was a time, metaphorically speaking, when you could more or less chap on the door of a hospital and get an operation. Those circumstances would alter dramatically, as I would painfully discover twelve years later.

But first things first.

In 2010 I was scheduled to do more work for the BBC's 'Sportsound' programme at St Mirren the Tuesday after I had first started to feel seriously unwell, much to my wife's disgust.

I thought I could ward off any symptoms I had by stuffing as many Nurofen into my mouth as I could but I distinctly remember Mhairi telling me I was a fool to myself to even contemplate the notion of going out to a football match on a winter's night to speak into a microphone and then reel away to bark like a dog when I was off air.

If I remember correctly, she emphasised her displeasure by storming off with a pile of ironing and a steely determination to let me do to myself whatever I foolishly wanted without an ounce of sympathy from her.

If I was stupid enough to play games with my health then that was my own fault, and that triggered something in my mind as I could feel my situation worsening by the minute.

I called Mhairi upstairs and told her I'd called the producers of the radio show to tell them I wasn't able to work that night due to unforeseen circumstances and she telephoned Dr Paul Jackson in a hurry for a rapid consultation.

Paul had been Dumbarton's doctor when I started out as a player at the club and had then gone on to work for Rangers. He was a good friend, and you can take it from me that, at a time when you're starting to get worried about your inability to breathe properly, club rivalries don't enter into any conversation.

An X-ray showed I had an enlarged heart and Paul assured me that was fairly commonplace in the case of sportspeople but, at the same time, he feared something more sinister was going on and urged me to go to Glasgow's Western Infirmary right away.

I didn't want to worry Mhairi unduly, but when I told my wife I wanted her to drive us there on a wintry night and over icy roads I think it must have alerted her to the gravity of the situation. Because that wasn't a set of events I would ever have considered under normal circumstances, if you get my drift.

Our time in the Western Infirmary wasn't long because I found myself being quickly dispatched into an ambulance while the paramedics put on the blue light and had a frantic discussion over the quickest way to negotiate the journey from there to the Golden Jubilee Hospital in Clydebank, renowned for its outstanding work on patients with heart problems. That's when the professional instincts kicked in because the former football manager in me caused me to attempt to sit up in the ambulance and tell the driver the short cuts between Partick and our final destination.

Before I knew it we were there and a camera was immediately put down my throat while an operating theatre was made ready for a sudden arrival who had no time to waste.

I spent three weeks in the hospital after my operation, six days of which were spent on a ventilator, and I owe my life to a now retired heart specialist, Mr Vivek Pathi. Mhairi went to thank him after my surgery and he had to interrupt her in full congratulatory flow because he was on his way to perform another operation to give somebody else a second chance at life. You can only stand back in awe at that kind of expertise and dedication, but how could I repay this wonderful man for returning me to my wife, children and grandkids?

I did exactly what he requested. Mr Pathi ran a boys' football team and his biggest wish was to have the experience of a complete training session for them at Rangers' training complex in Milngavie on the outskirts of Glasgow. As the former Celtic player and assistant manager of the team who had stopped Rangers from winning Ten in a Row, it was lucky for me that Walter Smith was the manager at Ibrox. I had known Walter since our time together at Dumbarton, when I was the teenage hopeful and he was in the twilight of his playing career. When he subsequently came down to Glasgow from coaching Dundee United to be Graeme Souness's assistant manager at Rangers, Walter and his wife, Ethel, became near neighbours of ours in Helensburgh.

They were a great source of comfort and support for Mhairi during my heart problems and when I asked for Mr Pathi's team to be given the run of Rangers' training complex, Walter was everything I knew he would be in terms of generosity with his time and interest.

Years later, Mhairi and I did what we could to be of assistance to the Smith family when Walter was diagnosed with cancer and tragically passed away on 26 October

2021. You have to be there for each other in this life, regardless of which side of one of football's greatest club rivalries you are on.

I had reason to understand that was the case when I encountered my second fight for survival less than a year after Walter's passing.

Endocarditis is, as I now understand only too well, a life-threatening inflammation of the heart's inner lining. It became the complication that affected me when I went back into the Golden Jubilee Hospital for the replacement of the heart valve which had been inserted twelve years earlier. And that complication ultimately led to eight weeks on a ventilator, a time of real concern for my wife and family as I fought for my life. I was back to looking over the edge and wondering if I would make it back from the precipice.

Originally, I had been told my case wasn't considered to be an emergency and my operation kept being put back as a consequence. To fill in my time in hospital while I waited to be operated on I was doing seven thousand steps a day in the grounds of the building as well as my stretches and sit-ups. I was like a player in pre-season training, doing what I could to build up my body to withstand the rigours of what lay ahead of me. I wanted old habits to die hard so that I didn't.

But the delays were getting to me and at one stage I contemplated calling the whole thing off and going home. That fit of pique only lasted as long as it took the medical people to tell me these were post-pandemic times and, if I left, I'd go right back to the end of the queue for surgery.

So, I went back to my training regime.

Show me a challenge and I like to think I'll demonstrate the mentality which insists nothing is going to beat me.

The operation eventually went ahead on 9 September 2022, and when endocarditis made matters much worse, I spent eight weeks on a ventilator while my life hung in the balance. It was, with no exaggeration whatsoever, a traumatic time for me and my recovery is still not yet complete.

What I have managed to do so far in terms of my convalescence does not constitute a victory in my eyes. My professional life was about wins and losses. What I am engaged in now is a fight-back and, like always, I'll work with every fibre of my being to get there in the end.

That's the story of how I got to where I am today. The story of the road that was travelled from Dumbarton to Celtic Park and from there into the Bundesliga with Borussia Dortmund, before coming back to Scotland and managing at Partick Thistle and Celtic, is the one I really want to tell. The days when you made your own luck and stood, or fell, by what you did to determine the difference between victory and defeat.

2

You're in My Heart

IN 2010 I WAS ON A FERRY, crossing the Swan River, in Perth. That's the Australian city which bears the name and not the one in Scotland where St Johnstone play their home games.

I was on my way to meet one of Celtic's immortal Lisbon Lions. Someone who had been part of my professional life since the very first day of my career in the game.

And in a never-to-be-forgotten kind of way.

Those were the kind of thoughts that were absentmindedly running through my head as I took in the beauty of my surroundings and floated across the water taking me from one side of the city to the other.

My moment of quiet reflection was suddenly disturbed, however, when I heard a booming voice with an unmistakably Scottish accent shout out, 'I don't believe it, Murdo MacLeod.'

The gentleman in question was an expatriate Scot and a lifelong Celtic supporter. The spontaneous hug he gave me was the kind you indulge in with a long-lost family member after years of separation. Except that I had never seen, or met, the man in my life before.

We were bonded due to the fact that I had worn Celtic's jersey for nine years and, no matter the fact that he lived on the other side of the world, the club was still close to his heart in a way that made distance an insignificant matter. That's why I know the saying about there being a Celtic family is no cliché. It is a statement of fact on a global basis, as that impromptu embrace in Australia illustrated only too well.

It lasted what seemed like five minutes, but the emotion was tangible, and I have always felt humbled by the affection I have been on the receiving end of over many years.

When I was on a ventilator following my heart operation in 2010, my daughters opened up a Facebook page and ten thousand people came on to offer their best wishes for my full recovery.

Ten thousand people.

Think about that and you begin to understand how a football club can be like a supportive family.

The girls used to sit at my bedside every day and read out the messages to me while I was fighting to stabilise myself. You can have no idea what that's like unless you've been in that position, and the memory of being sustained and strengthened by the support from the fans will live with me forever.

The Lisbon Lion I was going to see that day was Willie Wallace, who had emigrated to Australia when his playing career in Scotland was over. And, in fact, my own road to Celtic Park began on the day I met 'Wispy' for the very first time.

Milngavie, where I was born and brought up, would be categorised as one of Glasgow's posh areas, but I lived in a council house, went to the local Clober Primary School and subsequently attended the nearby Douglas Academy.

I appreciated very early on in life that the academic world was definitely not for me – not once I realised I had a talent for being able to play football and could hold my own against boys who were much older than me.

I have always had a mind of my own into the bargain, which is why I ended up signing for Dumbarton, eventually moving from there to Celtic, when there were a host of more exotic names, including Rangers, who wanted me to join them instead. As a young prospect, you were invited to spend time at the clubs that were showing an interest in signing you, and for me that meant visits on both sides of the border.

Crystal Palace, for example, were so keen on me that their then manager, Malcolm Allison, used to come to my temporary digs in the capital and drive me to training every day in his Mercedes. Big Mal was one of the most flamboyant personalities the British game has ever seen, all fedoras and cigars and dolly birds, as they were known then. He was a national celebrity, for goodness' sake, and there he was driving a sixteen-year-old from Milngavie around London.

But I knew instinctively that Palace weren't the right club for me, so I had to disappoint the most famous chauffeur I have ever had and move across the city to sample Arsenal next.

The club immediately brought me into their iconic old ground, Highbury, full of marble flooring and busts of Arsenal's legendary figures in the foyer. It was a common ploy used by football clubs to turn the heads of the young and impressionable so that they would sign on the dotted line when terms were offered. The trick might even have worked if I hadn't been an innocent bystander caught up in the Knickerbocker Glory scandal.

I was put up in a London hotel with a host of other hopefuls and everything was going well until the club discovered that meals and delights like the infamous Knickerbocker Glories were being ordered and then charged to Arsenal's account. Everyone, me included, was sent home as a punishment, in spite of my absolutely truthful defence that I had never even heard of a Knickerbocker Glory, far less put one on their tab. So, Arsenal lost me to a dessert I had never tasted and I came back to Scotland to receive an invitation to go to Rangers.

They took prospective signings into the actual first team dressing room at Ibrox and you got changed in there before going across the road to the training ground known as the Albion.

I'd never seen, or heard, anything quite like the manager who was barking out instructions to the players and slaughtering the ones who weren't carrying out his orders properly. This was Jock Wallace, who had once been a jungle fighter during his days as a professional soldier and took his combative bearing on to the football field with him.

I wasn't frightened of him, and I wasn't too scared to turn down the offer of a contract that he made to me on a face-to-face basis. I had simply taken a look at the number of players who were already at the club and understood the difficulty I would have faced getting caught up in the traffic and never finding a route into the first team there. I wouldn't have been the first youngster to get lost in the crowd at a football club.

So that's why I could have gone to Crystal Palace, might have ended up at Arsenal, rejected the chance to join

Rangers and finished up signing for the Sons of the Rock at Dumbarton.

The manager at the time was Alex Wright and he told me that if I signed for him there and then I'd go straight into the reserve team for the game against Dundee, away at Dens Park the following night. I had the offer to be a professional footballer in twenty-four hours' time and my independent state of mind insisted this was the club for me.

Sure enough, the next day I found myself sitting on the team bus while going along the M8 motorway to Tayside when it made a swift detour at Cumbernauld. One of the other players got on there and he was, like everyone else in my company, new to me.

I'll always remember there was a first-team game going on at Dundee United that night and the roar of the crowd carried across Tannadice Street and echoed inside the almost deserted Dens Park. It sent shivers of anticipation down my spine.

I was eventually brought off the subs bench for the second half and told to replace the guy who'd got on the bus at Cumbernauld. But my outstanding recollection of that night came from the team bus journey back to Glasgow.

We detoured to Cumbernauld once again for the player's drop-off and when the man I could now legitimately call a teammate got off I asked the person next to me the question that had been troubling me all night.

'Who is that guy?' I said.

'That's Willie Wallace,' was the reply. 'He was one of the Lisbon Lions when Celtic won the European Cup in 1967.'

Astonishingly, I had made my professional debut by taking the place of one of the most iconic figures in Scottish football.

Willie and I laughed about that when the Swan River ferry dropped me off to see him and we still laugh about it to this day.

★

Despite my dedication to the game, life wasn't all about football. I played over one hundred games for Dumbarton, a journey that takes a teenager to manhood after learning to deal with more experienced players on a weekly basis. And when my time was up there, I made the club a lot of money in the transfer fee Celtic paid for me. It's what's called a mutually beneficial arrangement of the type that makes the football world go round.

It was three years of my life that served as an apprenticeship which would stand me in good stead for the remainder of my career, and I am still welcomed with open arms whenever I go back to watch the Sons play, which I frequently do.

The club has moved from the old Boghead ground where I learned my trade and now has more picturesque surroundings in the shadow of Dumbarton Rock, but the memory of that time in the original setting stays ingrained on my mind. And the bruises earned when I learned my trade are still felt to this day – it could be a pretty brutal apprenticeship! Dumbarton introduced me to the physical side of the game, which it most certainly was in those days. Definitely a learning experience!

The town of Dumbarton also introduced me to the woman I can safely call my better half. It could be argued that it's perhaps not the most romantic of settings, but it was the starting point for a marriage that has lasted decades and produced three girls and the grandchildren they have brought into the world for Mhairi and me. And I didn't meet my future wife on an exotic night out that would have put us into the category of Posh and Becks mixing with the glitterati from the worlds of football and showbusiness.

Instead, I actually met Mhairi in a garage where she was working behind the counter and having to deal with young upstarts who were intent on trying out their best chat-up lines on the good-looking girl at the till. Fortunately, my attempts to woo her met with success!

Mhairi and I got married while I was still a Dumbarton player and we bought a house in the town not far from their famous old ground, Boghead. The house didn't have a telephone and the moment I'm about to describe predated mobiles, so when the doorbell rang and I opened it to find the club's manager, Alex Wright, standing there I wondered what was wrong.

He said, 'You need to get to Celtic Park straight away. We've agreed to sell you to Celtic and Billy McNeill's there waiting for you to sign the contract.'

You could easily say it was the moment that changed my life, but that didn't alter the fact that not only did we not have a phone, we didn't have a car either. So, Mhairi had to get her mum to come over to the house and pick me up to get me to Celtic Park for the biggest meeting of my life.

Of course, even though events were moving incredibly fast, I knew exactly what was happening and it was hugely exciting. Alex had told me who I was meeting, but when big Billy walked into the boardroom my mouth quite genuinely fell open.

I reverted to type in that moment. I didn't turn to anyone for advice. I didn't ask for time to think over the offer. I just took the pen and signed the legal paperwork in front of me and then stepped out into the street as a Celtic player.

I made my first team debut for Dumbarton against Queen of the South on 18 May 1974. I married Mhairi on 11 June 1977. And I signed for Celtic on 2 November 1978.

There are dates which are emblazoned on your mind because of their importance and the effect they have had on your life.

Those are mine.

The following day I went to the Hiram Walker distillery in Dumbarton, where I had worked while playing part-time football for the Sons, so that I could say goodbye to the people I knew there.

I noticed that those who supported Rangers were giving me a wide berth and I understood in that instant I was now part of a club rivalry which divides a city in particular, and a country in general.

I was now part of a club that would cause people on the other side of the world to become overwhelmed by emotion when they met you by chance on a ferry in Australia.

Within months of signing for Celtic I would be involved in a single match against Rangers that would be described by some Celtic supporters as the greatest night of their lives and by others as having provided a moment which ranked alongside the day when Inter Milan were beaten in Lisbon and Billy McNeill became the first British player in history to lift the European Cup. Big Billy always said there was a fairytale aspect attached to Celtic and it is true.

'Ten Men Won the League' became a phrase which would enter Celtic folklore and my winning goal on the night would be enshrined as the greatest ever scored by a Celtic player in an Old Firm derby.

The whole experience of playing for Celtic shaped my life. If I'm asked to pick out a single moment or a game that defined my time at the club I can't give a truthful answer other than it was a privilege to have been part of something so special. Every day of every week of every month of every year that I was there.

My time at Celtic was bookended by Ten Men Won the League and, two decades later, being assistant manager to Wim Jansen when Celtic won the title and stopped Rangers from winning Ten in a Row at the same time.

Wim became a major figure in Celtic's history on the day that we beat St Johnstone with goals from Henrik Larsson and Harald Brattbakk. He couldn't go anywhere in the world after that without Celtic supporters coming up to him and thanking him for what he had done for the club.

Wim's funeral took place on 29 January 2022 and Mhairi and I attended the service in Rotterdam. When the coffin was brought into the room the Rod Stewart song 'For the First Time' was played respectfully in the background because it carried a strong emotional attachment for Wim and his beloved wife, Coby, dating from the first time they had met.

As the funeral cortege passed by outside the Feyenoord Stadium where Wim had been a player, red flares flew through the sky, propelled there by the fans. And at that moment we were hugged by Celtic fans who had come from Germany to pay their last respects. That's what it means to me to have been part of Celtic for so long and to have known, and continue to know, the extent to which you are held within people's hearts.

We came back from the funeral and went to the first home game played at Celtic Park after returning. Mhairi told me she had seen Rod Stewart go into the boardroom, and that was an opportunity I couldn't miss because it was important to put him in the picture concerning the service for Wim.

When I came out of unconsciousness in hospital after surviving the complications caused by heart surgery in 2022 there was a card on my bedside table. It was signed by Coby and all the members of the Jansen family. On the front of the card it said, 'You'll Never Walk Alone.'

That is what it is like to be held in the embrace of the Celtic family.

3

For Wim

THERE WAS A POST-MATCH ritual which had to be observed after every home game in the season when Wim Jansen, with me as his assistant manager at Celtic Park, stopped Rangers from winning ten league titles in a row by beating St Johnstone 2–0 on 9 May 1998.

The management and coaching staff from whoever we were playing would go into Wim's office for the traditional hospitality that followed the final whistle.

And then, once they had left the ground, Wim's wife, Coby, and my better half, Mhairi, would come in with Wim junior, his daughter Petra, and our three girls, Mhairi junior, Gilan and Marina.

Wim's kids came over from Rotterdam for every home game in that incredibly dramatic season and they loved the atmosphere inside Celtic Park.

But a song had to be sung before we went our separate ways on a Saturday night:

There's only one Wim Jansen.
Only one Wim Jansen.

He's got curly hair. We don't care.
Walking in a Jansen wonderland.

Outside the front door at Celtic Park there were two sets of fans living in a fevered environment, almost paralysed by the fear of what might, or might not, happen about the championship.

But inside the stadium there were two families who had bonded when our working partnership began, and that human relationship kept us cocooned and immune from the pressures of the outside world.

Wim was the best I ever worked with and yet he had arrived in Scotland to be faced with a tidal wave of apathy and downright hostility. There was even one newspaper headline which said he was the 'worst thing to hit Hiroshima since the atomic bomb'.

Wim had been head coach at Sanfrecce Hiroshima before joining Celtic.

It was an awful, and deeply insensitive thing to say about anyone. If only for the reason that the atomic bomb dropped on that Japanese city on 6 August 1945 in the final days of World War Two had taken the lives of tens of thousands of people. You can't mention an atrocity like that in the context of a football tournament. But Wim somehow managed to rise above it all.

By the time he left Celtic ten months after reading that headline, he had made himself an iconic figure in Celtic's history. I thank God Celtic gave him the job in the first place because I shudder to think what might have happened in that highly pressurised time if a lesser managerial talent had been chosen instead of Wim.

We developed an instant connection from the first day we met during a pre-season training camp in Holland and also formed a personal understanding which lasted from then until the day Wim died, having lived with dementia, in 2022.

Wim was too dignified, composed and disciplined to be distracted by the personal insults that were thrown at him following his arrival from Japan. I cannot recall him ever confronting any journalist over what was written, or said, about him. Not even after we lost our first two games of the season, away to Hibs and then at home to Dunfermline, and there were calls to the Radio Clyde phone-in from Celtic supporters demanding Wim got the sack before it was too late and the unthinkable happened in the title race.

Two games.

On the day that we played the thirty-eighth game of that season, a 2–0 win over St Johnstone that stopped the Ten for Rangers and won the most exciting and daunting championship I had ever known, it was a different story altogether.

You can imagine, or if you were lucky enough to have been there to witness the moment for yourself, you will know what it was like when the referee blew his whistle to end that game. The months of pent-up emotion, the fear and trepidation which had gripped the Celtic fans vanished in an instant. A tense, highly charged afternoon turned into bedlam and pandemonium, and that's a barely adequate description to sum up the outpouring of raw emotion and uninhibited joy.

The players took a thoroughly deserved lap of honour with Wim and me following on behind them.

I knew Wim was triggering a release clause in his contract which allowed him to go at the end of his one and only season with the club.

But I had also gained a comprehensive understanding of the man's capabilities and strengths by that time. And I knew that the players, to a man, had an overwhelming belief in him and his managerial methods.

So there, in the midst of the euphoria, the deafening noise, the tears and the antics of the people and the players who were cavorting for all they were worth, I thought I would give it one last try.

A final tug at the heartstrings.

I said to Wim, 'Look at all of this. Don't go. Change your mind and stay.'

He put his arms around my shoulders, flashed that terrific smile of his, and pointed to the fans.

'Murdo, what a way to go.'

And we were done.

If the fans could have heard that exchange it would have made the mood even more intense than it was.

We had to fly to Portugal for a friendly match with Sporting Lisbon two days after that game. It was a match that was as anti-climactic and flat as we knew it would be in the aftermath of the title-winning celebrations. It was an occasion as sombre as it deserved to be while we came to terms with losing the manager who had taken just ten months to become a Celtic icon. A legend for all time.

But in the quiet of the dressing room that night I could hear Wim hum one of football's anthems. The silence was broken and, when the players' ears became attuned to what Wim was humming, there was the mood swing to end all mood swings.

The song on his lips was 'Stand up for the Champions'.

One by one, the players got up and feet started to be stomped on the dressing-room floor while arms were linked.

We were the champions. Wim Jansen's champions. And this was, quite literally, our swansong. I've never heard that anthem sung with greater depth of feeling than it was that night. The shivers still run down my spine just thinking about it.

★

There was substantially more decorum on that first day we were introduced to Wim. I had been working at an SFA coaching course in Largs when I was approached by Celtic and asked if I would join them on an unspecified basis. Tommy Burns, another iconic figure in the club's history, had gone from the manager's office and Wim had to follow a much-loved and idolised figure. The threat of Rangers creating an all-time record for consecutive league title wins, and I use the word threat advisedly, hung in the air and dogged the footsteps of every Celtic supporter.

I stepped into that oppressive environment with my eyes wide open because I at least had an intimate under-standing of the Old Firm rivalry from my time as a player at Celtic Park.

Wim was having his appointment as manager mocked without anyone giving him an earthly when it came to succeeding, due to the fact he'd never even seen an Old Firm game, far less having the knowledge of what it took to win one of them.

To say the atmosphere was fraught with tension was no exaggeration, but on day one I found out a lot about the man I had been asked to form a partnership with while never having met him before.

Wim liked the way I coached the players and told me after just one session that he wanted me to be his right-hand man. I couldn't have been more pleased.

Every day from then on we would spend two hours after our coaching work had ended talking about Celtic's next opponent. There was no other topic of conversation beyond what it would take, step by singular step, to win the title for Celtic. We never discussed any aspect of Celtic's historic rivalry with Rangers other than how to overcome them on the field of play.

Wim openly contradicted the culture of Scottish football and, by being a League Cup and title-winning manager in one season at Celtic, he proved that he knew best when it came to his style of man-management.

He also created what I would regard as being an all-comers record for our domestic game by acquiring two trophies while never having had an alcoholic refreshment or uttering a swear word before, during or after matches.

I was by his side every day and I never once witnessed him lose his composure or celebrate any win, no matter how big and influential it might have been, with a drink.

Even when the champagne was flowing, he would be standing quietly in a corner of the dressing room. The only thing he drank in was the celebratory atmosphere because he knew we had made so many people happy with our work on the field of play.

I should have known.

When we were in Holland for our pre-season training camp ahead of a dramatic and traumatic championship, there was a game against an amateur team that we were winning by a ridiculous margin.

That didn't stop me jumping to my feet and screaming at the players to keep going, score even more goals and understand that they had to keep going to lift their fitness levels.

I'd heard the same advice shouted at me throughout my playing career and it came as second nature to me.

Then I heard a quiet voice behind me say, 'Murdo, sit down.'

Football, and what makes individual players and teams better, was Wim's game. Not histrionics.

★

The Celtic fans used to call the manager Wim the Tim, but he wasn't at all interested in the divisive aspect of the rivalry with Rangers, and to this day I have no idea if Wim was a religious man or had no faith at all. He didn't ask me about my beliefs and I never discussed the subject with him.

What I can tell you is that Wim Jansen looked after people. He was the perfect manager and a perfect gentleman. He was also a great family man who brought a different mentality to the job of caring for, and about, his players.

I'd been in dressing rooms where it could get a bit lively at half-time if things were not going according to plan during a match. But Wim would come in with no trace of panic in his demeanour and no intention of ranting and raving. There were no arguments, only calmly delivered instructions on what had to be done for the best.

And after those two opening defeats in the league, the best was what followed. Wim didn't get along with the

Celtic hierarchy, not the club's owner, Fergus McCann, and certainly not Celtic's general manager, Jock Brown. They were ultimately the reason why he left the club, but the manager never had any strained relationships with anyone inside the dressing room.

Jock was a well-known figure within the game. He had started out in print journalism and then moved into the world of television commentary on matches. He was a university graduate with a legal background and had a suitably imposing manner about him. Our paths rarely crossed because I was fully focused on doing all I could to help Wim settle into the club and get to grips with the job of preventing Rangers from winning a historic Ten in a Row.

I think it would be fair to say the Celtic supporters found Jock a difficult character to accept as one of them, and that was illustrated on the day when it was announced he was leaving the club. It was a match day and I'm told the atmosphere inside the ground could have been described as carnival.

Jock once infamously used the word 'traded' to explain Paolo Di Canio's move to Sheffield Wednesday and that upset the fans who adored the Italian in his one full season of creating unforgettable moments. They certainly didn't think he should be traded for any reason whatsoever.

Inevitably, there came a moment when our worlds eventually did collide and it happened when Celtic beat Dundee United at Ibrox to win the League Cup final. It was Wim's first trophy for the club and the fans' gratitude was obvious when the team bus arrived back at Celtic Park to find an adoring throng waiting for us there. To my seasoned professional's way of thinking, it was obvious that either Wim, the manager, or Tom Boyd, the captain, should have the honour of being first to emerge from the bus while holding the trophy aloft, always an iconic image on days like that. But it looked to me as if it was Jock who seemed intent on fulfilling that role and I felt compelled to offer my observations on the subject of right and wrong.

Ultimately it was the captain who did the honours and, rightly or wrongly, I thought that day provided the moment when my relationship with Jock went downhill with no hope of a U-turn.

I have had too many great times in my career to dwell on the less savoury incidents or get into the business of settling old scores. The season I had with Wim was, in particular, too filled with achievement and acclaim to let the memory be soured by acrimony.

In the end, I was called into Jock's office, after the league title had been won and Wim had gone home to the Netherlands, and I was told my time at Celtic was over and done with.

I left the club, but the club never left me, and I walk in the front door at Celtic Park with my head held high, assured of a warm welcome every time I go to watch the team play.

★

We had a multinational team. Henrik Larsson from Sweden. Enrico Annoni from Italy. Regi Blinker was from the Netherlands, and there were a couple of Danes, Marc Rieper and Morten Wieghorst.

Diversity had to be accompanied by an understanding of the localised issue we were dealing with at the time. I was from the West of Scotland and had an intimate understanding of the Old Firm's rivalry from my nine years wearing Celtic's jersey. My name had been made, to a large extent, on goals scored for Celtic against Rangers and careers are measured by how you perform in that Old Firm derby.

There's no point in saying the derby can play too great a part in people's lives. It is Scottish football's signature fixture and the reason why television pays for the global interest it creates.

We had, in amongst the continental contingent, Paul Lambert and Craig Burley. Neither had been brought up as Celtic supporters but, like so many names threaded throughout the club's history, they played for the jersey as if they had been born holding one in their hand. That was never better exemplified than on the day we had the festive fixture with Rangers which turned out to be the pivotal moment in that spine-tingling season.

'Burls' scored with a clever finish to a good team goal and then 'Lambo' almost ripped the net apart with a long-range effort that was stunning in its execution. The crowd went off their heads and Paul's reaction to the strike wasn't exactly sedate either!

Any season of that magnitude is made up of inexplicable moments, like losing the first two games of your season back-to-back, and unforgettable moments when the balance of power takes an unmistakable shift.

Every Celtic fan who left the ground that day knew they had witnessed a turning point and nothing had to be explained to the non-Scots when it came to increasing their understanding of what had taken place.

I had to be Wim's official translator at times, but that was mainly to help him understand the Scottish boys who spoke at machine-gun speed.

The only time he ever looked truly perplexed was when he was doing a defensive coaching class in front of a whiteboard and telling the players they had to stay on their feet in the penalty box.

There was widespread laughter in the room and Wim asked me what was so funny about the things he was saying.

I had to tell him that on television the night before they had shown a re-run of Archie Gemmill's goal for Scotland against Holland in the 1978 World Cup finals. The goal was voted the best one scored in that tournament and one of the Dutch players Archie had waltzed around before scoring was Wim, who was very much not on his feet and very definitely on his backside while being bypassed for the final strike.

Wim saw the funny side of it all but none of us were laughing when it finally came time to say goodbye and watch the manager return to the Netherlands.

There are elderly Celtic supporters who can recall the Scottish Cup final over Dunfermline in 1965 that was Jock Stein's inaugural triumph just weeks after becoming manager and consider it to be the birth of the modern-day version of the club.

Billy McNeill succeeded Big Jock and his winning of the league title by beating Rangers in our final game of the season will be the indelible moment in Celtic's history for those who were there.

Martin O'Neill's first derby win over Rangers, a 6–2 epic, would have left an indelible mark on the minds of those who were inside the ground that day, and that list would have included Noel Gallagher who was in Glasgow for an Oasis concert after the match.

Ange Postecoglou lost his first derby and then quickly got out of the habit.

Brendan Rodgers was brought up on Celtic while living in Northern Ireland and gathered an impressive record of wins over Rangers which puts his name in lights for the fans.

The point to all of this is that outstanding achievements recorded at the expense of your greatest rivals carries greater weight than anything else. That is just the nature of football rivalry the world over.

You might argue that Glasgow is a world of its own and Wim Jansen is, for that reason, an iconic figure for Celtic fans because he stopped the unthinkable from happening.

An old friend of mine, who was at the final league game of the season against St Johnstone that won the title, told me about some supporters who were crying tears of anxiety before the match started. Those turned to tears of joy by full time and then the fans constructed a pedestal on which Wim was placed for all time.

There wasn't a place he could go anywhere in the world without being greeted by expatriate Celtic supporters who would rush to demonstrate their gratitude for what he had done on their behalf. I saw it for myself many times and I knew how richly he deserved every word of praise.

Wim was such a modest man and the way in which he said farewell to Glasgow, his players and the other members of the Celtic management team was tribute to his unassuming personality.

Wim hired a private room in a Glasgow hotel and invited every member of his back-room staff, along with their wives, to a farewell meal.

The Last Supper.

He didn't make an emotional speech or anything like that because it wasn't his way of conducting himself. Wim asked each of us to come forward, one at a time, and then he presented us with a beautiful watch as a parting gift.

I still have mine now because it's a treasured memento of a special time.

We kept up our friendship after that. His first visit back to Scotland after leaving Celtic was to attend a surprise birthday party for me at a hotel on Loch Lomond.

I remember when the season was over and Wim left the club, I paid him a surprise visit in the Netherlands. I was back in Germany to buy a car and I drove to Rotterdam, where Wim lived and was back coaching Feyenoord's youth team.

He had been at a youth game and when he returned home Wim found me standing in his kitchen. It was a nice moment and when we sat down to start talking Wim showed me what I could only describe as a detailed collection of written thoughts on how the man-management of football players should be conducted.

All of this hand-written work would later be turned into Wim's autobiography, which started out as being for Dutch consumption only, but was later translated into English for the benefit of the Celtic supporters who bought the book in Scotland.

There was no detail too small to be overlooked and I suddenly realised this was the manual by which Wim had worked from day one at Celtic Park while guiding the team towards a championship win like no other.

For example, one part related to how players should be spoken to when you were asking them how they felt about any given situation relating to them.

There was one occasion when he asked me to approach Tosh McKinlay and Malky Mackay to establish how they felt about playing in a reserve match.

My upbringing in the game told me that a manager, or one of his assistants, would go to two players under those circumstances and tell them where, and when, they would be playing in a reserve match. I'd never heard of an invitation, able to be rejected if they wished, being extended to players in this way.

As it turned out, Tosh and Malky didn't fancy the idea and Wim had no problem with that because he took the view that they knew their bodies best and what did, or did not, suit them.

The next game they played, I thought the pair of them were exceptional and I realised Wim was right again.

Recreation during a season like that one was important, too, but Wim knew good downtime from the bad variety.

Craig Burley had asked to see the manager on the players' behalf to ask permission for a three-day team break in Spain. I accompanied him to Wim's office to see how he would handle that type of situation. He was sitting behind his desk with his glasses halfway down his nose and reading a newspaper when Craig made his sales pitch.

'The boys were thinking it would be a good idea to take a break in Spain for a few days, gaffer,' he said. 'Would that be okay with you?'

Wim looked up momentarily and simply said, 'No.'

One word. Two letters. Three bags full.

'That'll be that then, I suppose,' Craig said before turning on his heels and going back to the dressing room, where he opened the door and offered his impression of Wim.

'No,' he told the players, and that was the end of the matter.

Wim didn't adapt to our ways. We adapted to the way he thought the game's business should be conducted, as per his manual.

He wasn't trying to be a killjoy about the proposed Spain trip. His first thought was he didn't want the players taking undue risks, larking about and accidentally getting hurt on a night out. The season was too important for him to stand by and allow that to happen.

The players, and we had one or two 'characters' in our squad, totally bought into the Jansen philosophy. If they disagreed with anything he said, they discussed it among themselves. There was never any confrontation with the manager. They had the utmost respect for Wim and he would have done anything for them.

When Henrik Larsson's wife wanted to tend to her horses in the countryside where they lived, Wim's wife would babysit their young son, Jordan. Wim's wife understood football and he and she were never apart.

When Wim had his seventy-fifth birthday in 2021, Mhairi and I were honoured to be the only two non-family members to be invited to his celebratory meal in Rotterdam.

Wim was not in the best of health by that stage, but he enjoyed his evening and we spoke about that incredible time together in Glasgow with a mixture of emotion and affection.

He passed away on 25 January 2022 and we returned to the Netherlands for the funeral ceremony at Feyenoord's stadium. Mhairi and I were holding up well until they played two tunes.

One, as mentioned earlier, was by Rod Stewart, who was a particular favourite of Wim and his wife. One day when we were at Celtic together, Wim said to me, 'Do you like Rod Stewart?'

I replied, 'Yes, of course.'

Wim asked me if I liked Rod's recording of a song called 'For the First Time'.

I had to admit I had never heard of it, and he nearly exploded.

This was the song that was special to Wim and Coby throughout their lives together.

We went to pieces when they played it at the funeral and when they then played 'You'll Never Walk Alone', the emotional dam burst for us.

It made Rod Stewart well up, too, when I told him the story of that day in the boardroom at Celtic Park some time afterwards. I didn't recount the story with the intention of making him cry but he was visibly moved by what I had to tell him. He was in an emotional state in any case because we had just watched Ange Postecoglou's Celtic win an Old Firm game.

Rangers had lost 3–0 to Celtic that night but I had to find their then manager, Giovanni Van Bronckhorst, and pass on a message to him as well.

Gio had worked under Wim as a young player at Feyenoord and the words he spoke about him by way of heartfelt tribute when his fellow countryman died had touched Wim's family in a very deep way.

I just wanted Gio to know that his sentiments were greatly appreciated and even though he had lost the biggest game in Scottish football we stood for ten minutes and remembered Wim in conversation.

I'll always remember that gesture.

In the same way that I'll always remember Wim Jansen.

People often ask a random question like: what were the three greatest things to happen to you in your career?

My answer is always the same.

Playing, and scoring, in the 4–2 game against Rangers that won the league title for Celtic in 1979.

Stopping Rangers from winning Ten in a Row while coaching at Celtic in 1998.

And having the privilege of knowing, and working with, Wim Jansen.

A man who spent so little time at one club but cast a giant shadow because of what he achieved there.

When they compile the list of immortal figures to have managed Celtic, Wim's name will be there on merit, and deservedly so.

On our last meeting in Rotterdam, it was clear that Wim was unwell but he was on great form nonetheless and his parting words to me were, 'See you soon, Murdo.' Just three months later Wim's daughter telephoned me to say he had passed away.

Gone but never to be forgotten by anyone associated with Celtic.

We were all part of that Jansen wonderland.

4

For Murdo

By Wim Jansen Jnr

WHEN MURDO CAME OUT of a coma in hospital in 2022, his wife, Mhairi, telephoned my sister, Petra, to give her the good news. It was a very emotional time for all of us because we had grown close as families from the moment my father became Celtic manager and appointed Murdo as his assistant.

We had found Murdo's illness to be so distressing because it was happening not that long after he and Mhairi had attended my father's funeral in Rotterdam. I couldn't bear the thought of Murdo being ill so soon after my father had passed away.

I like to think the Jansen family is like the MacLeod family. We are humble people who don't want a fuss made of us and it was that shared approach to life which brought us close together in 1997. There was only one occasion when all of that was forgotten about, and that was on the day Murdo and my dad won the league title for Celtic in 1998 by beating St Johnstone at Celtic Park.

The week before that game, I had been watching Feyenoord play away from home against Vitesse in the Dutch league while trying to keep in touch with Celtic's game against Dunfermline at East End Park. I was delighted when I heard Simon Donnelly had scored for Celtic and then disappointed when Dunfermline equalised late on in the game. But then my disappointment turned to delight once again because I remembered I was going to Glasgow the following week with my sister to see my dad's last game as Celtic manager.

It was the same story all over again when we got to Celtic Park.

Henrik Larsson scored an early goal but then Celtic were under threat and St Johnstone missed an easy chance to score themselves. My mind went back to the previous weekend and the nerves got worse because a late equaliser on the final day of the season would have been so costly. I knew Harald Brattbakk's winning goal was so important to everyone because of the number of Celtic supporters around about me who were openly crying.

When the final whistle blew, I let my emotions get the better of me as well. I was in the Directors' Box but I forgot all about where I was and stood on my nice, clean leather seat to join in the wild celebrations.

The people at the club invited us to go on to the pitch and join the lap of honour that my dad and Murdo and the players were doing in front of the crowd. At first we said we wouldn't do it because we were not the kind of people who would bang our chests in any public display of excitement. I wasn't a Jose Mourinho! But then I thought about the once in a lifetime opportunity we were being handed and I changed my mind. I'm glad I did because it was an amazing experience and I can't believe so many years have passed since that moment. I vividly remember that lap of honour to this day.

There was so much tension throughout that season and I understood why that was the case. It was about ending nine years of hurt for the Celtic supporters, and the MacLeod family and the Jansens shared every moment of what was going on with regard to the team on a weekly basis.

We lived it together. The Great Season, as I think about it still.

I knew about the rivalry with Rangers but I didn't fully understand the impact it had on people's lives until we were all immersed in that championship.

We and the MacLeods were an inner circle in spite of being different nationalities and from different cultures. Both families had a tight connection with each other and with Celtic Football Club. That has endured the passage of time.

I was in my twenties when I watched the match that stopped Ten in a Row and in my fifties when I went to Glasgow for the twenty-fifth anniversary celebration of that achievement. But I was only twelve years old when I wore a Celtic shirt for the first time. My father was a youth coach at Feyenoord at that point and took me to Spain with him to see an under-16s tournament there. I travelled in the Hoops because I had bought the shirt in a sports shop in Rotterdam. I was mesmerised by the colours on the strip and the design.

My support of the club continued when Pierre Van Hooijdonk left the Netherlands to play for Celtic. And then, years later, my father told me out of the blue he was going to become Celtic manager. I had absolutely no idea until a possibility became a reality.

I said at my dad's funeral that I followed what he did in football as a fan as well as a son. It was like that for me at Celtic Park. I felt nervous for the team. I loved the atmosphere there. I knew the club had one of the greatest crowds in European football and I loved being part of it with my sister and Murdo's daughters.

There were only one hundred people allowed to attend my father's funeral because it took place during the Covid-19 pandemic, but the family had to have Murdo and Mhairi there. They are warm people. Likeable people. That's why Petra telephoned Mhairi immediately to give her the sad news when my father died. We are like one family.

And now it is Murdo who has had difficulties with his health. Football is important but not as important as Murdo getting well again. We want to see him do that because he is like family to us. A strong bond that was created by Celtic.

5

The 4–2 Game

THERE'S A CELTIC JERSEY with a reserved place inside my house. It has been there since 21 May 1979 and it will never be sold, auctioned, donated or removed. You could say it's been there for decades because it has sentimental value. I see it as symbolising the moment when I became a league title winner for the first time.

That was the night I was propelled to a different level in the eyes of the Celtic supporters. A fevered event which led me to understand that champions know no fear. It was the pivotal moment of my fledgling career and it came on a night that is woven deep into the fabric of Celtic's history.

The night of the 4–2 game.

You have to appreciate the monumental nature of an occasion when it is known only by the scoreline, and with no need for further explanation. Those who were there when Celtic beat Rangers in what was our final match of the season to become champions still talk about it and the memory is seared into the brain.

Those who weren't even born then have been brought up on tales of how what was alternatively known as the 'Miracle on a Monday' came to pass.

The 4–2 game has added poignancy for me, of course, because I scored the last-minute winning goal that sealed the deal. Wherever I go in the world I am thanked for that intervention and asked to relive the moment. I've never had to be asked twice.

I was twenty years old and the six months I had spent at Celtic after signing from Dumbarton had been chaotic. Billy McNeill's first season as manager after succeeding the most legendary figure at Celtic Park, Jock Stein, hadn't run smoothly to begin with and we were mid-table when a horrendous Scottish winter disrupted the fixture list. Football didn't resume properly until mid-March.

Our chances of winning the league looked remote at best and even more so when we lost to Rangers by a single goal at Hampden while Ibrox was being rebuilt.

Playing catch-up is always a difficult, but a player who'd left Kilmarnock to sign for Celtic in the same week I joined the club really came to the fore for us. I thought Davie Provan was a superb winger and his crossing ability was to become a feature of our gradual climb up the table.

Every game we played was a must-win occasion and when we went a goal down to Partick Thistle we were back to walking a tightrope, until Davie scored an equaliser and George McCluskey got the winner.

The pressure was immense every time we crossed the white line on to the park but in the second half of that season we kept proving that we were up to the job.

As the season headed for its climax, Davie was still playing a key role and provided the ball that Michael Conroy scored from to beat Hearts and set up the title decider with Rangers.

After a brilliant run, we were a point in front of our old rivals, but they had a game in hand. In those days it was two points for a win. This meant we needed to win at Celtic Park but Rangers would only need a draw to win the title on our ground. Never a pleasant thought for our supporters to contemplate but a delicious prospect for the Rangers fans if their team was successful.

It would be unthinkable today but the television technicians who were supposed to film the game that would determine the outcome of the championship threw a lightning strike hours before kick-off and the plug was pulled on coverage of the match in highlight form.

Arbitration, conciliation, maybe even an altercation, would guarantee no such thing could ever happen now in the era of multi-million-pound television contracts. But all that exists of the 4–2 game is some grainy footage in black and white.

That has never troubled me, even as the scorer of the winning goal, because the moment when I scored is there and it is replayed on social media every year on the anniversary of the match.

And what a match.

I can still relive it in my head, and when I do that it is always in glorious technicolour.

A good story needs a beginning, a middle and an end.

The script that night had Alex MacDonald opening the scoring for Rangers after only nine minutes and before we could get to half-time he was also involved in what threatened to be another nail in Celtic's coffin.

Alex was lying on the ground after a challenge and the late Johnny Doyle gave him a little flick as he passed by while telling him to get up and get on with the game. The referee had an entirely different interpretation of the incident and immediately sent off Doyley for violent conduct. Johnny could be a volatile character, but I honestly believe he was hard done by on that occasion.

My testimony wasn't taken into account, however, and the second half started with Celtic being a goal down and a man down as well. That's when Davie Provan rode to the rescue once more, providing the immaculate cross that big Roy Aitken turned into an equaliser with sixty-six minutes gone.

The thermometer was rising inside the ground and the mercury almost went through the roof when George McCluskey put us in front for the first time in the match eight minutes after that.

But if you're going to have drama you might as well have the kind that carries all sorts of subplots.

Two minutes after George's goal, while the ground was still reverberating to the celebrations which had accompanied it, Bobby Russell equalised and Rangers were once again back in pole position to become the champions.

We were then into the territory where anything was possible for either side and fate was playing games with the emotions of everybody who was bearing witness to an occasion that had taken on a mind of its own.

The Old Firm derby has always been a separate lifeform, a domestic game like no other in Britain, and this match was underlining that definition.

With five minutes left to play, a ball that was floated into the penalty area accidentally came off the back of Rangers' defender Colin Jackson and slipped beyond his keeper, Peter McCloy, who had come out to deal with the cross.

We were 3–2 in front, the clock was ticking down and the game like no other was living up to its reputation in spades.

If Rangers equalised once again, they'd be the champions. If we scored another one, Celtic would be champions. The third scenario was that if we kept possession of the ball and held on to what we had, that would carry us over the line.

Five minutes might as well be an eternity under those circumstances, especially when the crowd have hit fever pitch and you can't hear yourself think on the park.

When the ball came to me I knew the minutes had, however agonisingly, ticked away to the extent that there were two options now available to me. I could hold on to it and hope the final whistle sounded, or I could have a shot at goal. If I scored, there was no way back for Rangers. If I missed the target, but the ball flew over the bar, it would land in the Celtic end of the ground and, by the time it came back out from the crowd, the referee would have his whistle in his mouth.

They have a statue of Billy McNeill outside of Celtic Park, and another one in his birthplace of Bellshill, for a reason. Billy's love of the club was unmissable, and he was the man who always said there was a fairy-tale aspect to Celtic because of the dramatic nature of their progress on the big occasions. He had written most of the fairy tales himself, being the team captain who had lifted the European Cup in Lisbon in 1967 after the defeat of Inter Milan in the final. And then being the manager who had won a league and cup double to mark Celtic's centenary year in 1988.

But on this day, it was his first time around as Celtic manager, and this was the climax to his first season in charge. He was the man who signed me from Dumbarton and had trusted me with a first team place on a regular basis. And every day in training he would say to me, 'You keep shooting, Murdo. You keep shooting.'

Those words came into my head when the ball landed at my feet that night against Rangers. I knew I still had the power in my legs to go for broke and shoot, even if there would have been people in the ground who would not have wanted me to part with the ball in case it allowed Rangers to have one last chance at going up the park.

Nostalgia can play tricks with you sometimes. Estimates vary over how far away from goal I was when I scored the winner. I think I was roughly twenty-seven yards out. That's my story and I'm sticking to it.

Distance was no object, regardless of how far it was, because the ball flew into the net and the Rangers players and fans knew that was the end of what had been a remarkable story.

That goal was voted by the Celtic fans as the best one ever scored in an Old Firm match. I would have to say I got another one at Ibrox in a game in 1986 that finished 4–4 which wasn't bad at all, but it didn't carry the same joyous consequences that that fourth goal did.

I fully understand that time moves on and those who weren't around to see the 4–2 game might say the result of the fans' poll has been made inaccurate by events which have taken place since then.

Henrik Larsson is my friend and his goal against Rangers, when Martin O'Neill was Celtic manager and experiencing his first derby in 2000, would be put forward as a worthy winner of my title. Nutmegging a defender and then chipping the goalkeeper was the kind of audacious sequence of events that characterised Henrik's time in a Celtic jersey.

But I'm going to be arrogant enough to say that I think my goal still stands the test of time.

Colin Jackson, who's sadly no longer with us, said it was his favourite Old Firm goal. The reason for that being if I hadn't scored then his own goal would have been the one which won Celtic the title. And he had absolutely no inclination to be stuck with that distinction.

You only get an understanding of the magnitude of any occasion by what happens in the immediate aftermath. The Celtic dressing room was a madhouse after we'd beaten Rangers in such an incredible fashion.

Johnny Doyle was thanking me and hugging me for making sure his sending off wasn't responsible for costing Celtic the title. There were Lisbon Lions in there as well and then the door opened and in walked the chairman, Desmond White. I had never seen him in there before, but the bedlam gave way to silence as he addressed the room.

He told us that what had taken place in front of so many disbelieving eyes was the greatest moment the club had known since 25 May 1967 and the winning of the European Cup for the first time by a British club. And he was saying this in front of some of the Lions who had roared in Lisbon.

You can't beat that for a compliment.

In the midst of the mayhem I also remember having a private moment with big Billy. He told me how much my goal would endear me to the Celtic fans and how glad he was he had always reminded me to keep on shooting.

I was as high as a kite but didn't have a drop to drink. I drove Mhairi and me home and I remember being so excited I started to talk to myself in the car, repeating over and over that I was a champion and would know no fear from that moment on.

The following day I went back up to the Park, just to wallow in the residual atmosphere of the crazy night before, and Davie Provan joined me for a photograph in front of the portrait of Jock Stein that hangs inside the ground.

The 4–2 game goes with me everywhere because there are always people who want to talk about it, relive the moment and reflect on the second greatest night in Celtic's history.

Stopping Rangers from winning Ten in a Row was the best moment I ever knew as a coach.

Winning the title against Rangers in the last game of the season was my top moment as a player.

Ask anyone who was there.

6

Stopping the Ten

I WAS ONCE GIVEN A CONDUCTED TOUR of a submarine when I lived near the Ministry of Defence base at Faslane on the lower reaches of the River Clyde. In the season when Wim Jansen and I were charged with the responsibility of stopping Rangers win ten league titles in a row, the atmosphere that hung in the air above us was such you wondered if we might need to ask for political asylum on the sub in the event of failure.

You need to have been born and brought up in the West of Scotland to fully understand the claustrophobic nature of the rivalry between the two clubs and the extent to which it preoccupies the lives of both sets of fans.

I once spoke at a dinner in Edinburgh where the audience was made up of Hibs and Hearts fans and when I was asked to name the biggest accomplishment of my career, I responded by saying the league title win that stopped Ten in a Row. Wholesale disbelief, not to say incredulity, came back at me. They couldn't believe that someone who had played for Celtic and Borussia Dortmund in the Bundesliga, as well as representing Scotland at a World Cup in Italy in 1990, could say such a thing.

When players born in Scotland are joining Celtic or Rangers they know the shape, size, colour and smell of the rivalry and are allowed to say they are 'living the dream' when they become part of it.

Contemplating the fallout from a nightmare is another matter altogether when you're at the sharp end and about to be submerged in hot water in order to see if you can pass an endurance test like no other.

There are lines you can't cross in the Old Firm's ring-fenced world. You have never seen, for instance, a Celtic player swap jerseys with a Rangers player, or vice versa, at the end of a derby, no matter how epic the match might have been.

And you never will.

I was on friendly terms with lots of Rangers players, but I would never have exchanged jerseys because the Celtic fans would not have appreciated the gesture.

I even turned down the offer to become the first Celtic player ever to leave the club for Rangers because I couldn't have done that to the supporters who were so good to me. And, in any case, it certainly wasn't something I wanted to do.

John Greig was Rangers' manager at the time, and I was approached by a third party to sound me out over the possibility of changing sides. My contract at Celtic Park was due to expire and I knew I was admired as a player by the Ibrox management. But the Celtic fans had taken me to their hearts. I couldn't do it to them or to my young family who would have had their lives badly disrupted by my actions.

I don't recall ever getting hassle on the streets of Glasgow because I was a Celtic player. At the same time, I wasn't going to take a temperature check on public opinion, or public disorder, by trading the Hoops for a Rangers jersey.

It would have to be a considerable amount of money to entice a player into crossing what they refer to as the Great Divide in Glasgow. But there are some things that are beyond price, and being able to look yourself in the mirror is one of them.

I couldn't have done that if I had taken all I had done at Celtic and performed the equivalent of throwing it all in the dustbin by going to Ibrox.

It might sound melodramatic to those who aren't immersed in the world of Old Firm rivalry, but players are ostracised and have their names expunged from their club's history if they are perceived to be traitors.

What I did by refusing to get into any conversation about joining Rangers had nothing to do with a dislike of the club. I acted out of personal respect for the Celtic supporters, not disdain for any individual on the other side.

I have never hidden my friendship with the late Walter Smith, and never would, because he was such an outstanding human being and richly deserves to be immortalised in stone outside Ibrox.

My main motivation was to honour the club and the supporters who had meant so much to me, and still mean as much to me to this day. I'll never know what Rangers thought was the price of acquiring my services at the end of my Celtic contract because I refused to enter into negotiations on the subject.

But I did know the price of becoming what would have been viewed as a mercenary in the eyes of the supporters. Voluntarily giving up one club's jersey for that of their greatest rival would always be seen as an act of betrayal.

Five years after I rejected that idea, my old teammate at Celtic, Mo Johnston, had no such hesitation. He arrived back from playing football in France with the original intention of rejoining Celtic, the only club he had ever wanted to play for, as he had said in public at the time, only to sign for Rangers instead.

It was as if a tragic disaster had taken place leading to widespread suffering inflicted on the Celtic support. They were wounded by a sense of betrayal.

I had been in the team with Mo on the day in 1986 when we went to play St Mirren on the last day of the season and won one of the most dramatic league titles ever in the history of Scottish football. With minutes left to play, and Celtic five goals in front, we were still fated to finish in second place because Hearts were goalless against Dundee and the Edinburgh side only needed a draw to be crowned champions.

Seven minutes later, Dundee had scored twice through a player called Albert Kidd and the pitch in Paisley was invaded by ecstatic Celtic fans who mobbed Mo, me and any other player they could get their hands on.

A few years later I attended a function to celebrate the anniversary of that extraordinary day. Footage of the game was shown and the ticket buyers on the night, who were exclusively Celtic fans, started to boo when Mo scored each of his two goals.

I had to appeal for order and say it would never be acceptable for me to stand by and listen to a Celtic player being booed in that way. If we hadn't scored enough goals that day, the title wouldn't have been won because the title was won on goal difference.

Mo had done his bit for the team.

He did what suited him best when he eventually joined Rangers from Nantes and he did that, I believe, because exceptional money can speak extremely loudly in transfer negotiations.

That's how professional football works.

The other side of that coin, or thirty pieces of silver as the currency was in the eyes of the Celtic fans who called Mo 'Judas', is the price of overturning more than a century's worth of tradition.

His name was removed from Celtic's history in the eyes of the fans the instant his name went on a contract at Ibrox. That's the way the rivalry works. In or out. All or nothing.

So that was the backdrop when we started the job of stopping the Ten by playing Hibs at Easter Road in the 1997/98 season. Fans who are suffering from nervous anxiety can be led to believe that twists of fate are the strongest indicator of how things will turn out in the end.

We lost in the capital because the winning goal came from a misplaced pass by Henrik Larsson that was smashed into our net by Chic Charnley. Chic was the biggest Celtic supporter in Glasgow never to have played for the club he adored, and he never hid his allegiance. His goal celebration that day involved running directly towards the Celtic dugout and shouting at me.

'Tell him I'm a Celtic man,' he was screaming by way of asking me to inform Wim that the green and white jersey he had on wasn't necessarily the one he preferred to wear. It was a verbal request for a transfer to the place of his heart's desires right in the middle of a football match. That's how much Chic wanted to play for the Hoops.

It was also a brutal start to a league campaign with severe demands on us.

And it got worse.

We lost the next game at home to Dunfermline and a cultural and emotional clash took place in the Celtic dressing room after the final whistle.

Wim spoke to the players about our 2–1 defeat. I blasted them.

The foreign way, I had discovered, was to ask for things to be done. The Scottish way is to demand that they be done. Or else.

I stood up, raised my voice, and screamed, 'We are Celtic Football Club. We don't lose at home to Dunfermline.'

I don't believe I was being disrespectful. I was being realistic. It was a spontaneous outburst and Wim had no problem with me. You might have called it a case of good cop, bad cop. I called it getting players to understand that I knew they were capable of much better than they were delivering on the field.

No points from a possible six. The fans in despair. There was no time to be lost and no margin for error.

I have to assume the message lodged in the players' minds because we won our next eight games on the bounce. And then promptly lost to the one team we had to beat in order to avoid disaster. Rangers beat us at Ibrox due to a solitary goal from Richard Gough, but the one positive to emerge from an otherwise negative afternoon was the debut made for us by Paul Lambert.

Paul had been a Champions League winner with Borussia Dortmund, my old club, the season before, and he was a quality addition to our team.

The Dortmund fans loved me because I was a thief. I stole the ball from the opposition and set us in motion. Paul's game was to receive the ball, hold it and pass it on with maximum effect while generally being a figure of authority in the middle of the park.

And at Celtic he cemented his reputation by scoring a magnificent goal against Rangers in the next Old Firm derby at Celtic Park that sealed a win started off by Craig Burley's goal.

Burley, Larsson and Lambert. They were the firm of architects who drew up the blueprint of our title win. But the story had more twists and turns before the job was done.

On 12 April we went to Ibrox with five games of the season left to play. Jonas Thern and Jorg Albertz scored the goals for Rangers that not only won the game but put them on top of the league table on goal difference.

But the best plot twist of the lot had still to come.

The penultimate round of games had Rangers playing Kilmarnock on the Saturday, with us away to Dunfermline twenty-four hours later.

Rangers' game was refereed by a man whose leanings towards the club had long been highlighted by the Celtic support and, in a world of suspicion and conspiracy theories, the worst was feared by those of a cynical disposition developed over a long period of time.

The regulation ninety minutes came and went at Ibrox without a goal for either side, and those who believed in the possibility of jiggery-pokery, for want of a better description, felt that the award of a penalty to Rangers might be the inevitable consequence of their inability to put the ball in the net any other way.

Then there was a fact-is-stranger-than-fiction moment.

Not only did the referee not give a penalty and materially influence the outcome of the match, but Kilmarnock scored in time added on – additional minutes that exceeded the length that might have been reasonably expected in either half of the match.

Rangers had shot themselves in the foot and sustained a potentially fatal, but self-inflicted wound.

The case against the referee, Bobby Tait, was found to be Not Proven.

Celtic, on the other hand, were guilty of premature celebration after we'd gone a goal up on Dunfermline through Simon Donnelly. And when we bent down and waited for the league championship medals to be placed around our neck, the home team kicked us up the backside.

Dunfermline's Craig Faulconbridge hit us with a goal from nowhere with eight minutes to go. The party hats and streamers had to be put back in the box and we were left to steel ourselves for the final day, potentially a winner-takes-all match at home to St Johnstone.

I had to hope the rant I had directed towards the players after the second game of the season had stayed vivid in their minds. St Johnstone is a fine football club, but they shouldn't be standing in Celtic's way when we have home advantage and a league title is at stake.

Henrik Larsson's early goal should have calmed our nerves, but it didn't because of the intensity of the occasion.

St Johnstone's George O'Boyle really should have equalised for them but he misdirected a header over the bar.

It took a late goal from Harald Brattbakk to settle the match, and the nerves, while cancelling any need for a request to re-enter a submarine on the Clyde for sanctuary.

Mhairi says I had a fish supper when we went home and then retired to bed. I have no recollection of that happening but I know I had no alcoholic refreshment. I wanted to keep the memory of that day in particular, and the season in general, clear in my mind.

It had been the most intense period I had ever known in my life. I went to bed the victim of mental exhaustion. But Wim and I did what we had been asked to do and therefore sleep came easily to me.

I'm not sure Ten in a Row will ever be done by either half of the Old Firm.

Celtic have got to nine titles in succession on two occasions, with Rangers having done it once. Jock Stein managed Celtic to the first nine, but times were different then in respect of the fact that managers had a longer shelf life at any club.

Graeme Souness started Rangers' nine but he left for Liverpool because that was what he wanted, and Walter Smith won the vast majority of their titles when he succeeded him.

A succession of managers were responsible for Celtic's second arrival at the cusp of Ten in a Row but I always suspected their chances had diminished when Brendan Rodgers upped and left one morning to go to Leicester City.

The Celtic fans are still not over that decision to trade the possibility of immortality, in their eyes, for what they regarded as mediocrity in the Midlands.

Loyalty, however, can be a two-way street, as Wim and I discovered after stopping the Ten.

7

The Old Firm

STOPPING RANGERS FROM WINNING Ten in a Row was the most meaningful of the achievements I had racked up against Celtic's biggest rivals as player and coach. I had been fortunate enough to have scored goals against Rangers that had won a League Cup final at Hampden and a league title at Celtic Park, but the championship win had to be put into historical context.

The Old Firm rivalry, as it was known then, was a cultural phenomenon. As it remains to this day. The match between the two sides divides a city, a country and a global audience of expatriates who care as deeply about the outcome as anybody else.

Stopping the Ten meant no revision of history, and that's crucially important to supporters who detest being overtaken when it comes to the record books.

Jock Stein had won the original Nine in a Row to cement his legendary status among the Celtic fans. Rangers had retaliated in kind before the combination of Ronny Deila, Brendan Rodgers and Neil Lennon put together another Nine in a Row after the millennium.

Territorial superiority means everything to the fans.

The players of both sides at the time when I signed for Celtic were almost exclusively Scottish, brought up in what was called the Great Divide and driven by the demands of an intense rivalry.

The late Colin Jackson, a Rangers defender on the night in 1979 when I scored the winning goal to win the league title in what became known as the 4–2 game, told me that was his favourite strike in any Old Firm game. As I recounted earlier, Colin said what he did because it meant he would not go down in history as the Rangers player who had won the title for Celtic. He'd had the misfortune to put the ball into his own net and put the game 3–2 in Celtic's favour, but my goal had diverted attention away from that moment and provided a different focus of attention.

That was how much it meant to him and it's a classic example of what the Old Firm rivalry means to the players and the fans. A mistake in any other game would be talked about and forgotten. In an Old Firm game, however, nothing like that is ever forgotten and it will be talked about for years, sometimes decades. It's something the players know only too well and is yet another thing that heightens the tensions in those encounters.

What Wim Jansen and I had achieved by stopping Rangers from getting a tenth successive title was some-thing that reverberated far and wide and I never tire of discussing what happened that day in particular, or that season in general.

But there was one man who never spoke to me about it and who knew I would never raise the subject with him for personal reasons.

The man in question had been a veteran player at Dumbarton when I was there as a raw teenager, happy to learn off him and the likes of John Cushley, a former Celtic centre half who was also part of my football education.

I had moved to nearby Helensburgh with my young family after signing for Celtic and, when my playing career was over, my mentor of many years earlier, who lived close by in the town, was a friend I could visit to watch football on television or have as a dinner companion with our wives.

But there was one topic of conversation that was taboo.

The man's name was Walter Smith and he had been Rangers' manager on the day I helped deny him footballing immortality.

I knew what I had gained and Walter had lost the day we beat St Johnstone at Celtic Park but there was too much mutual respect for me to be anything other than mindful of his feelings.

Walter was the Rangers man who was so loved by my late, great teammate, Tommy Burns, that the family asked him and another Ibrox legend, Ally McCoist, to be pallbearers and carry his body into St Mary's Catholic Church when cancer tragically took him from us in 2008.

It would never have occurred to Walter to think twice about agreeing to that request from the Burns family in case anyone else raised an eyebrow over his decision.

Just as there was never the slightest hesitation on my part to sign for Celtic when they asked me to leave Dumbarton for them.

Part of the cultural aspect concerning the phenomenon that is the Old Firm is that boys who had attended Douglas Academy in Milngavie were supposed to have been destined for Rangers, not Celtic, if they had the ability to reach that level.

That thought never crossed my mind, just as it had not influenced legends of the club like Kenny Dalglish, Danny McGrain and a host of others who brought distinction to Celtic and loved every minute of their time there.

On the day, or night, when Celtic played against Rangers it wasn't about the school you attended or any other aspect of your background. It was about giving everything for the jersey, or the badge as modern terminology would have it.

I knew there were guys in the Celtic dressing room who were wrapped up in the history of the club because they had been brought up on stories of great triumphs and players who had gone into folklore.

It was never more evident than when we were about to play Rangers. How could it be any other way when we were managed by Billy McNeill, the living embodiment of all that Celtic meant to the people who supported the club.

Every steward, kitchen worker, handyman or electrician who worked for Celtic would stop you for a word before you could get into the dressing room to change for the match against Rangers.

The message was always the same and could be summarised by saying that defeat was not an option that could even be contemplated.

The derby gets to people like that.

My wife, Mhairi, was heavily pregnant on the night we beat Rangers to win the league at Celtic Park, but she recalls one of Johnny Doyle's uncles whirling her around when I scored with absolutely no regard for prenatal protocol.

Doyley was such a big Celtic man he didn't even like to play for us at Ibrox. Just being inside Rangers' ground had the effect of unnerving him.

The Celtic players' wives didn't go to Ibrox for our games there and it was a reciprocal arrangement when Rangers came to Celtic Park. That's why I know Mhairi was in the house doing the ironing and listening to the game on the radio, or wireless as it might have been then, when I equalised in the game that finished 4–4 at Ibrox in 1986.

Families become immersed in it all. They know the songs and what it is to take the club to your heart.

I remember our youngest daughter, Marina, bringing the house down at a music event in Ireland when she took to the stage and sang a great Celtic fans' favourite, 'The Fields of Athenry'. She was all of eight years old at the time and the event happened to be in Athenry.

Throughout my career I would get Rangers fans coming up to me and saying, 'You should have signed for us.' There was never any malice involved and I always took their words as a compliment. The greater your personal achievements against Rangers, the more it enhanced your reputation in the eyes of the Celtic supporters.

They wanted more than anything else to see players who battled hard and fought to win every challenge in a derby match, and I like to think that's why they appreciated my efforts in that direction.

There was no banter on the park between the players of both sides and no fraternisation afterwards in a social context. But I never saw any reason why you couldn't respect each other as people at the same time.

That's how it was between me and Walter.

We kept a discreet distance between us throughout that season when Wim and I were striving to win the title with a historical significance that would resonate with the fans.

And when it was all over, and Celtic had won a championship as famous as any in their litany of successes, there was never any likelihood that I would let partisan feelings get the better of me in Walter's company.

There were no words necessary in the first place.

I knew that what I had helped Celtic achieve was monumental in the eyes of the club and those who wished us well. I also knew, from a professional standpoint, the scale of the disappointment Walter had suffered as a consequence. You let it go at that.

Walter was a good man, a decent man who was always great company. I would go round to his house when he was diagnosed with cancer and it was hard for me as a friend to watch his health gradually deteriorate.

Ethel, Walter's wife, was one of the first faces I saw in my hospital room when I finally regained consciousness after spending eight weeks letting a ventilator breathe for me and bring me back to life.

There's a game and there's real life and you have to allow yourself a sense of perspective at times without letting that dilute your sense of pride in your club.

8

The King of Kings

A N EPIC CELTIC STORY BEGAN with a single sentence.

'I think I know someone,' Wim Jansen said to me when we sat down to talk about what the side we had inherited in 1997 needed to make it roadworthy for a journey through a season that carried tremendous significance for the club.

The sentence Wim spoke comprises two monosyllables and three other words. A throwaway line.

By the time the season had ended we were talking about someone who had almost drained the English language of the superlatives used by his admirers to describe the contribution he had made to Celtic.

The someone Wim knew was called Henrik Larsson.

If you became known in word and song as the King of Kings then the chances are you must have been doing something right, and Henrik could do no wrong in the eyes of the Celtic supporters.

It is testimony to just how idolised Henrik was that two decades after he left Celtic Park to go to Barcelona, he is still held in exactly the same high regard. The people who loved him then still love him now, and with absolutely no reduction in the strength of their affection for him.

That won't be the case with the modern-day players. They pass through the club's history, illuminating it briefly and then the memory of their time fades after they move on elsewhere.

Henrik was at Celtic for seven years, during which time he managed to become the third top goalscorer in the club's history with 242 goals in 313 games. Only Jimmy McGrory from the pre-war era and Bobby Lennox have more goals to their name, but in terms of total goals scored and goals per game, Henrik Larsson's contribution is astonishing.

It helps when you become the biggest single factor in preventing Rangers from winning Ten in a Row in your first full season in Scottish football, of course. And when your goal to help beat Dundee United in the League Cup final at Ibrox in 1997 gives Wim Jansen his first trophy as Celtic manager and boosts the morale of the team who would go on to win the title.

But Henrik arrived to sign for us as a top-class player who then became a world-class player, and they don't come along two at a time like buses.

I have to be perfectly honest and say that when Wim told me his name in our first conversation about him I'd never heard of Henrik. Wim knew everything, from the break-out clause in his contract with Feyenoord to the size of the fee it would take to get him to Glasgow to who acted as his agent.

The fee of £650,000 didn't suggest we were getting an outstanding talent, but it told us everything about Wim's judgement. He knew the player was undervalued to the extent that the transfer fee would later be seen to be the equivalent of robbery in broad daylight.

Today you could go to your video analyst at any club and ask him to research any player and you'd be given the visual version of a dossier that ran to the length of a novel. But that facility wasn't available to us then, so initially I thought we were taking a bit of a shot in the dark.

The club moved quickly, as they had to do under our pressing circumstances, and in an upstairs office inside Celtic Park a couple of days later I clapped eyes on the Swede whose friends called him Henke.

He walked into the room with his wife and agent while he carried his infant son, Jordan, in his arms. The charisma that came off him was enough to fill the building, never mind that one room. He made the floodlights look dull by comparison. The dreadlocks, the hair band, the way he looked and talked, the man was an identikit photo of what a superstar should look like.

Downstairs in the dressing room we had Craig Burley, who took out his two front teeth before we played matches, and I say that in jest only to underline the overwhelming feeling I had that something special was about to hit the club.

The team photo was about to be improved for sure, but Henrik was more than a man who oozed charisma and glamour. This was a guy who did his shift. Whether it was on the training pitch or in a competitive match, he grafted and chased people down as well as being a superb finisher in front of goal.

He also had that continental ability to put things into perspective without letting any form of adversity interfere with his confidence. If a Scottish player had passed the ball straight to an opponent in his first match for his new club and the opponent had then lashed in the winning goal by taking advantage of that gift, there might have been what we call a head in a bucket.

But Henrik rationalised everything calmly and quickly.

Sure, he'd made a mistake, but you simply resolve to be better the next time you play. It's not the end of the world, because the games roll into one another.

The first time I had concrete evidence of that being the case, and Henrik's philosophy being proved to be the right one, was when we went to play St Johnstone in Perth on the rebound from two league defeats that had fans' fingers hovering over the panic button.

Henrik played a one-two with Simon 'Sid' Donnelly and then took himself into a position inside the penalty box that he knew could be telling if Sid's cross was accurate. The ball sent in was a model of precision and Henrik threw himself full length to meet it with a glorious header that sent us on our way to a comforting, and comfortable, win.

When players are in a dressing room and they look at someone like Henrik there's an aura that rubs off on them. They believe they're in the presence of someone special and they know he's a game-changer.

Your very own Superman without the cape.

But he wasn't the journalists' dream ticket because Henrik was a private individual. He didn't much care for talking about himself and he didn't do many press conferences. But he wasn't in any way aloof or someone you would call a Billy Big-time when he was in the company of his teammates. He liked to socialise with them and opened up in their company.

The only time there was a whiff of controversy was when Henrik and Tosh McKinlay had a fall-out on the training field in the week of a game against Rangers. The press reaction was what you might expect; banner headlines about what Henrik might do and speculation that a return to the continent might be uppermost in his mind. But I can tell you that was never going to happen.

Henrik was outraged by what had taken place but the situation was temporarily defused because he had to go back to Sweden to attend a family funeral. Time away from the ground allowed him the space to calm down and he returned determined to be the perfect professional and move on for the sake of the team.

I wouldn't attempt to deceive anyone and say relations between the two players were restored. For the rest of my time at the club they kept their distance from each other.

The only way I got involved was when it was suggested to me there might be grounds for dismissal, where Tosh was concerned.

I was close to Henrik and what happened was definitely unacceptable on the training pitch, but my sense of fair play told me the subject of dismissal couldn't be based on some sort of celebrity justice system.

Henrik might have been more famous than Tosh and more revered in the eyes of the fans, but I saw no merit in punishment being decided on the basis of a popularity poll.

The regrettable incident involved a coming together in the heat of the moment. It has probably been replicated in grounds the length and breadth of the country over a long number of years, but it clearly didn't leave Henrik disillusioned because he was at Celtic Park for another six years after it happened.

It was the club's great good fortune that Henrik loved the city of Glasgow and so did his family. He enjoyed what he achieved at the club and I know that because we are still in regular contact to this day. He doesn't call me to check up on my health or anything like that. He calls for an update on what's happening at Celtic Park. Wherever he is in the world, Henrik is a long-distance Celtic supporter.

He showed his undying affection for the club when he scored against Celtic when Barcelona was his team and there was a Champions League tie to be won. The professional instincts kick in at moments like the one when Alan Thompson was short with a pass-back and Henrik pounced in his trademark, and predatory, way.

He was respectful of that when his celebration of the goal he had just scored was muted to say the least. There was never going to be an extension of his arms and that trademark tongue being stuck out, and I think the Celtic fans appreciated that he was never going to rub their noses in a goal against their team.

Where you get into sacrilegious territory is when you try to establish Henrik's place in the pantheon of greats to have walked through Celtic's gates, as the supporters' song says.

There will be people of a certain generation who will have a special devotion to Jimmy Johnstone or Kenny Dalglish and say they were without peer in a Celtic jersey.

And then there was that jocular question of whether Henrik would have got a game for the Lisbon Lions. The retort was always that he could have taken Jim Craig's place at right-back and, to be fair to big Jim, he always takes the jibe in good spirit. The reason for that, I think, is that Jim can always content himself with the knowledge that he is, was, and always will be enshrined in history. As a Lisbon Lion.

You can say what you like and accuse me of letting personal interest get in the way and I won't deny it, but, for me, Henrik will always be the number one.

The King of Kings.

9

The Heart's Desire

DEEP DOWN IN MY HEART of hearts I always hoped that I might be Celtic manager one day. I'd spent nine years playing for the club and been assistant manager there in a season that brought a glorious distinction. The thought of completing the circle and taking up the ultimate job was in my deepest subconscious.

When you play for, or coach, a club of Celtic's size there is always a huge emotional investment in their well-being that consumes your entire family. My daughter, Mhairi, was a ball girl at Celtic Park throughout the season we stopped Rangers from winning Ten in a Row by becoming league champions. If you look at any photographs from the post-match celebrations which followed the final-day win over St Johnstone, the chances are you'll see my three girls not far away from Wim Jansen when he's holding the championship trophy.

And their mother was equally committed to the cause.

On the day in 1986 when we had that incredibly dramatic league title win by beating St Mirren in Paisley, while Hearts slumped to defeat in Dundee, Mhairi was the only player's wife to turn up for the match because she, like me, had never given up on the hope that the improbable was not necessarily the impossible.

If I had been a plumber there might not have been moments when I'd go home and find my children in tears because of something related to my job. But I'd still much rather have played for Celtic than been a plumber spared domestic strife because of what I achieved with, and for, the club.

That old cliché about football being a funny old game is inaccurate, though. It's a brutal old game.

I didn't get to be the manager and achieve my dream. I had to leave the club in 1998.

I still remember how it felt on an emotional level.

I walked past the receptionist in the foyer and she was in tears. I kept my head down and walked on towards my car outside the ground. The impact of what had happened took a long time to subside and not even the World Cup finals in France could offer a distraction and take away the pain of separation from the club I love.

Before I could even get to France and begin my job of assessing Scotland's opponents for Craig Brown, the national team manager, I had to go home and tell the women in my life that I was no longer a Celtic employee. It's hard for a parent to take when his kids are distressed.

Football clubs are places of work, and there isn't one of those anywhere I know where everybody enjoys cordial relations with everyone else, especially in a high intensity environment where you have a football team carrying the hopes and expectations of a global following.

There was never a serious disagreement behind the scenes and away from the dressing-room area. There was never any interference from outwith the football department when it came to team matters. But on the day Celtic won the League Cup final on 22 November 1997 by beating Dundee United 3–0 at Ibrox, there was an exchange between Wim and our general manager, Jock Brown, on the team bus when it arrived outside a predictably crowded and excited Celtic Park.

As mentioned earlier, Jock was about to exit the bus while holding the trophy when Wim intervened and said he felt the team captain, Tom Boyd, should have that ceremonial honour. He felt that was football's way of doing things and I had to agree with him that an unnecessarily awkward moment had occurred.

The cup was put down in the place from where it had been lifted and thereafter we had a great night, as I recall.

I took no special satisfaction from winning the trophy on Rangers' ground. I would have rather tradition was observed and we won it in front of even more of our fans at Hampden Park. It was more important to me that the events of the day proved we had a team of winners, and when the second tangible sign of superiority came in the form of winning the league title, I felt vindicated. Even if the moment moved me closer to the day I cleared out my desk.

Wim had decided to trigger the release clause in his contract and return to the Netherlands. Before I could retrieve those dreams of becoming manager from my deepest subconscious and bring them to the forefront of my mind, I was told I was leaving the club as well.

A phone call summoned me to the general manager's office and a brief conversation informed me that a new management team had been assembled and was on its way.

Football's like that. It's all part of the game.

Wim and I had replaced Tommy Burns and Billy Stark. Doctor Jo Venglos and Eric Black succeeded us until they were out in favour of John Barnes, who was eventually overtaken by the charismatic figure of Martin O'Neill and a new era began.

You go into this game with your eyes wide open and I will forever say it was terrific for me to be part of Celtic Football Club. They meant everything to me, and still do.

As the song says, don't look back in anger. Instead, remember why you get hugged by total strangers in any part of the world you visit because you gave them a moment they will never forget.

I had no argument with the club's owner, Fergus McCann. We had just one meeting in my season on the management staff and that was about win bonuses. He was the most businesslike man I ever met in football.

Fergus could separate emotion from efficiency without a second thought. He seemed to regard chasing trophies and, more importantly, stopping Rangers from winning Nine in a Row under Walter Smith as short-termism. The big picture was to rebuild the club financially and reconstruct the ground to make it a fit place for the Celtic supporters. He put his own money on the line and removed the family dynasties who had historically held control of the club.

Fergus even stipulated the timescale he would need to carry out all of his plans before going back to America with whatever personal profit he had made. I, nor anybody else, could have no problem with any of that because of the legacy he left behind.

Hindsight is a wonderful thing and I believe McCann's efforts are more greatly appreciated today than they were at the time.

I certainly bear him no personal grudge.

★

I left knowing I had worked with a special managerial talent in Wim Jansen, someone whose memory resonates with me when I look at Ange Postecoglou. Wim and Ange came in when there was reconstruction work needing to be done so far as the team on the park was concerned. Both brought a cool focus to their work, and each of them bought in good players to get the work done.

Other than that, I can only find one word to describe what it was like to no longer work, or play, for Celtic.

HORRIBLE.

10

Home and Away

I WAS BORN AND BROUGHT UP on the west side of Glasgow. I had played for nine years wearing a Celtic shirt in the East End of Glasgow. And I was living with my wife and two daughters in Helensburgh. In other words, I was living out my professional and my private life in a thirty-mile radius and I was approaching my thirtieth birthday.

But I wouldn't be telling the truth if I tried to say I moved to the Bundesliga and signed for Borussia Dortmund because I wanted to broaden my horizons, embrace a new culture and learn a different language. I left Scotland and uprooted my family for reasons that were entirely pragmatic.

Dortmund made me a financial offer that was life changing and I couldn't possibly have turned it down.

The first thing I had to do was establish how much I was being offered because the financial terms were explained to me in Deutschmarks. The Euro was still some way off back then and I needed to go away and find someone who knew about conversion rates.

It was the kind of money I couldn't have hoped to have earned in Scottish football and the offer came at a time when the testimonial match I thought I was going to get for ten years at Celtic had been thrown into doubt.

Testimonial matches were a traditional way of providing long-serving players with a nest-egg for the future, so the loss of one gave me fresh food for thought about how I was going to provide for my family.

My mind was in turmoil because Billy McNeill was coming back in to manage Celtic, and there was no figure associated with the club I respected more than big Billy.

I had to be completely honest and truthful with the man who had signed me from Dumbarton and shaped my career. I told Billy exactly what I was going to get for going to Germany and he put my feelings before all other considerations. Even Billy, the manager who had looked after me at the pivotal moments in my life, refused to stand in my way in order to suit his personal requirements.

The big man did put his feelings into more graphic words.

'You've got to take it,' he said. 'We'd be farting against thunder trying to compete with that kind of money.'

If a man such as he refused to deny me a once-in-a-lifetime opportunity, then I knew I could leave Celtic having been open and honest with everyone and respectful to the club who had made me the player good enough to attract the interest of Borussia Dortmund.

It was a time of change at Celtic Park. Davie Hay was to be replaced as manager, but Billy's arrival back at the club in 1987 for the start of a season that would incorporate the club's centenary year had yet to be formally announced.

I was on a family holiday in La Manga when I received a telephone call from a players' agent in Germany, Bruno Klier, advising me that Dortmund were keen on bringing me to the club.

Two days later I got another phone call, but this time it was from someone representing Eintracht Frankfurt. They also wanted to make me an offer.

The coincidence was that both clubs were due to play a match which would decide, based on league placings, who would qualify for a place in the UEFA Cup the following season.

I was flown from La Manga to Frankfurt for that game and was immediately struck by how much the travelling support from Dortmund reminded me of the Celtic fans with regard to the level of noise they made and the fervour they obviously had for their team.

Dortmund won the match 4–0 and, after further negotiations, I left my holiday in Spain for a second time and gave my commitment to sign officially for the club at a later date.

In the meantime, Billy was back in his rightful place as Celtic manager for a second time, and he called me to find out where I stood with regard to the immediate future. It wasn't easy for me to tell the man who had brought me to Celtic Park from Dumbarton nine years earlier that I was going elsewhere but I had a perfectly frank conversation with him.

And when I revealed to Billy the size of the financial package I was to receive from Dortmund he had only three words to say by way of a response.

'On you go.'

He assured me there would never be any bad feeling between us and that he understood my personal circumstances.

Billy being Billy, he went out and signed Billy Stark from Aberdeen after I had gone, and Starky promptly scored the only goal of the game in the first derby of the season against Rangers. A benchmark moment on the way to the winning of the league championship.

I was twenty-nine years old. I had a wife and two daughters of primary-school age. I wasn't in any way betraying the club where I had made my name, but I would have been betraying my family if I hadn't taken the opportunity to guarantee our financial security. An offer like the one from Dortmund was unlikely ever to come up again if I let it pass me by.

So, I flew to Germany to complete the deal that would take me a long way out of my thirty-mile radius but Mhairi, my wife, wanted to stay behind at first so that she could attend her father, Peter's, birthday party.

She had one of those intuitive feelings about her dad's health and, sadly, Mhairi was proved correct. Peter died soon after the family get-together and it was a stark reminder that you never really know what's in front of you in this life. I would have ample cause to understand the accuracy of that statement once my playing days were over.

On 24 July 1987, Mhairi and the girls flew to Germany to join me in Dortmund and a memorable period in our lives, as well as my playing career, began.

We stayed in the city's Lenhoff Hotel to start with while we looked for a place to stay and it was there I got to understand the difference in lifestyle as a player I was experiencing. The entire squad and our head coach, Reinhard Saftig, would stay at the hotel the night before Dortmund's home matches at the Westfalenstadion.

When it came to having dinner for the first time together, I was astonished to find the players were told they couldn't have a Coke with their meal, but they could have a beer. And when we gathered socially after our dinner at nine o'clock to have a chat before bed, the players could have another beer, but Coke was still verboten. It made no difference to me because I was strictly teetotal then and always had a cup of tea.

But things didn't go better with Coke in Germany, in spite of what the commercials on British television said at the time. German beer had a lower sugar content than Coca-Cola and too much sugar wasn't good for the players, so it was a strictly enforced ban and nobody stepped out of line.

Similarly, when it came to house-hunting, I would always specify that I wanted a garden. I wasn't fluent in the language then and something may have got lost in translation but the impression seemed to be among the estate agents we dealt with that I wanted a garden for the purpose of growing vegetables. Eventually, though, we found one man, Wilfred Shtamm, who understood I only wanted a garden where I could watch the kids grow up as part of a contented family.

And so the MacLeods of Helensburgh became the MacLeods of Werl-Budberg, a nice location that was a thirty-minute drive along the autobahn for training at the Rote Erde stadium that was Dortmund's second home.

It was there I was introduced to the fans for the first time at an open training session, complete with piper brought in from a nearby army barracks housing British soldiers.

I was always comfortable with German football because it suited my style of play, and the aggression I brought to the team was greatly appreciated by the supporters.

I knew I was always under special scrutiny because I had come in from another country, but Reinhard Saftig was the kind of coach who spoke to you rather than shouted at you and I got on well with him.

My German was getting better as well because my younger daughter, Mhairi junior, had one night told off my teammates in our hotel. Some of the players would ask to come to our room so that I could help them learn better English, but Mhairi said that had to stop and told them they could only converse with me in German since I was the one member of her family who wasn't up to speed with the language yet.

I knew enough by September of that year to fully understand what was being said on the radio about the draw for the UEFA Cup. Dortmund had been drawn against Celtic and the first leg was to take place in Glasgow.

I couldn't believe it.

Celtic had never before been drawn against German opposition in any European competition and it had to be against my team a matter of weeks after I'd signed for Dortmund.

I was going back to the place I regarded as home, but I was going into the away-team dressing room. It was a home and away match for me on the same night.

I didn't know quite what to expect, but what happened that night on 15 September, in front of what was an all-ticket crowd at Celtic Park, was one of the most emotional homecomings I had ever known.

Mhairi and the girls had flown back to Glasgow for an occasion they couldn't possibly miss and they also sat in the Celtic end of the Directors' Box to keep up tradition. When I was a Celtic player and we were at home, the girls always sat on the knees of Mary and John McStay, the parents of Paul, Willie and Raymond.

The ovation I got from the old Jungle before kick-off was something that will always live with me.

Derek Whyte snatched victory for Celtic on the night with a last-minute goal, so the mood of the crowd was lifted no end.

And yet it was my name they chanted after the final whistle had sounded. It was just like the old days as 'Murdo! Murdo!' echoed around the ground. It was all too much for me by that stage and I left the pitch in tears.

The Dortmund fans listened to what was being sung and from then on that was the chant that followed the announcement of my name before every game at the Westfalenstadion.

Big Billy had looked for me that night and we had a private moment where he hugged me and congratulated me on making myself a fixture in the Dortmund team so early in my time at the club.

That meant a lot to me.

We won the return leg in Germany, scoring two goals without reply, so the reception I got from the Celtic fans that night was more muted. You don't go chanting the name of one of the opposition players if they've just put you out of Europe.

I understood the ground rules and will always carry the memory of the scenes before and after the game at Celtic Park in my mind.

★

Playing, and living, in Germany was an experience I look back on with immense satisfaction. I'm glad I made the move abroad and I would always have regretted not going there.

I still have the commemorative T-shirt the club produced when we won the German Cup by beating Werder Bremen and I'll get to the peculiar end to that particular day later on. But that wasn't the only souvenir I brought back to Scotland with me when my time was up in the Bundesliga.

I think I might be able to lay claim to the fact that I am the only former footballer from Scotland to have two bricks from the demolition of the Berlin Wall upstairs in the loft at my home in this country. I had them brought back to Scotland in the truck that carried our worldly goods when we left Dortmund in 1990 so that I could sign for Hibs.

My wife and I, along with the two daughters we had then, enjoyed assimilating ourselves into the German way of life. And we were greatly helped in that regard by one of our neighbours, a lovely woman called Monika Wimmeler, in the village where we lived outside of the city.

Monika and her family could tell us what life was like after World War Two and Germany was divided into East and West, a political move symbolised by the construction of the Berlin Wall in 1961.

East German guards manned the wall and, over three decades, more than one hundred people lost their lives by being shot as they tried to rejoin their families in the West.

I watched British television by satellite at home in Germany and used to tell my Borussia Dortmund team-mates what was being said outside of their country about the removal of the wall in the days leading up to 9 November 1989.

By an amazing coincidence, Dortmund were playing a game in Berlin on 9 November and we went back to our hotel in the city and watched the television coverage of people literally demolishing the wall with their bare hands amid tremendous scenes of joyful celebration.

The Dortmund players were cheering as they watched the beginning of their country being put back together again and it was hard not to get caught up in the moment along with them. It was a moment of historic significance and just being in the city made you feel part of a world-altering event.

I felt even more part of it when I returned to our home and had a visit from Monika. She had felt so moved by the reunification of her country that she had driven from Dortmund to Berlin, a considerable distance that the team had covered by aeroplane, and had removed bricks from the detested wall to keep for posterity. And she wanted the MacLeod family to have a couple of them to remind us that we were living in Germany when history was being made.

I wouldn't have been so dismissive of anyone's feelings as to leave them behind when we left the country, so we made sure they were part of our luggage.

The wall I remember best after the one removed by people power was, coincidentally, also in Berlin. It was the outer wall of the Olympiastadion, where Dortmund had beaten Werder Bremen 4–1 to win Borussia their first trophy since 1965. That was on 24 June 1989, five months before the protesters dismantled an unwanted symbol of separation.

I was kept back that day, along with my teammate, Frank Mill, for the urine test that was part of the anti-doping measures in football. The pair of us, along with two Werder Bremen players, sat there for so long until we could properly carry out the test that the German guys had actually started to have a drink and a cigarette to pass the time.

By the time we did what was necessary to satisfy the medical people, it was so late they had closed the stadium, so there we were at the perimeter wall of the ground in pitch darkness and with no telephone to alert anyone to our predicament. There was nothing else for it but to climb over the wall and drop down to the other side as part of our very own Great Escape.

Somewhere in Berlin, ecstatic Dortmund fans, players and officials were having a party, and we were wondering how to join them. Luckily for us, someone from the club had the foresight to organise a car to wait outside the stadium and pick up Frank and me so that we could join the shindig. And I'll always have the medal and the recollection of scaling a wall to remind me of the day the cup was won.

When I was brought to Germany and delivered to my first coach at Dortmund, Reindhart Saftig, he had a new player to work with minus any detailed knowledge of what I was good at on the field. But he, along with his successor, Horst Köppel, knew that the fans liked me because I was a fighter.

Landmark games, and what followed, cemented my reputation.

There was a time, for example, when one of the club officials was having a party at his home on the day we were playing Bochum and he was naturally anxious for us to win so that the occasion wouldn't fall flat. I scored the only goal of the game and then I surprised everyone at the party afterwards by turning up in full Highland dress. I'd had the kilt and everything that goes with it made in Scotland and sent over to me at our home in Dortmund.

We didn't go to Germany to be insular. We deliberately sent our children to a German school rather than one for British people only so that they could assimilate themselves into the culture. But I wanted to show everyone I was proud of my national identity too, and the outfit went down a storm, even if there was a preoccupation among my teammates to find out if it was true what they said about Scots and what was worn, or not worn, underneath the kilt.

When I went back to Dortmund for the twenty-fifth anniversary of the German Cup win, or before that for the one hundredth anniversary of the club being formed, I always made a point of returning in full Highland dress but only speaking the German language.

No one in Dortmund could ever do enough for me and my family and I will never forget that, or the 'Yellow Wall' area of the Westfalenstadion, where the supporters took me to their hearts.

I was there as a fan when Dortmund beat Real Madrid 4–0 in a Champions League match, and that was when I first met Jürgen Klopp during his time as head coach. He came up to me after the game and embraced me like a long-lost friend. Jürgen knew what I had done with the club and was very generous with his praise for me. It made that climb over the wall at the Olympiastadion all the more worthwhile!

★

Homesickness was never a problem for me in Germany. I liked everything about the country and I admired the football there as well. It was, in all sincerity, a cut above what I had been used to in Scotland and I don't know what would have happened with the rest of my career if it hadn't been for the introduction of the Three Foreigner Rule by UEFA.

Today you might find only three Scottish players in Celtic's team on any given match day, but in those less cosmopolitan times it was decided to limit the number of players who weren't born in the country where they played their football.

I didn't want my place in the team to be partly dependent upon the country of my birth and when I started to be on the bench for the start of some of Dortmund's games I went to the coach, Horst Köppel, who had replaced Saftig a couple of years earlier, and told him I was unhappy. I could accept not getting a game if I wasn't playing well, but I couldn't have politics influencing team selection.

I was disappointed at having to leave Germany and Köppel later admitted in interviews that he had made a mistake in not putting up a greater fight to keep me.

I'd played in 103 league games for Dortmund, won the German Cup and the Super Cup and was sad to go. But I left the country content in the knowledge that Germany had made me a better player and, to be blunt about it, had done my bank balance no harm at all into the bargain.

Such is the life of a professional footballer.

The only thing I regretted about my time in Germany was that I wasn't able to be part of the league and cup double which decorated Celtic's centenary year in 1988.

I did get back for one match, when Celtic scored five goals at home against Dundee on a day when the crowd was so vast they had to move people around the still largely unseated ground in order to maintain crowd safety.

I did a bit of radio work that afternoon and when the first goal went in from Chris Morris I have to admit I let out a yell which prompted the studio to ask if I could keep calm in case any listener objected to favouritism.

Old habits die hard when you've worn the jersey!

11

Branco File

THERE WAS A TIME when I did the after-dinner speaking circuit telling stories of my career at club and international level spanning several years and just as many countries. It was a hopefully jocular insight into the parts of the game the fans don't get to see but always like to hear about.

There was one story I used to tell which stood the test of time in terms of audience reaction, even decades after the actual incident I was describing took place. But I don't think I'd repeat it now if I was out on the road because of the sadnesses which have taken place as a result of the subject matter involved.

The year was 1990 and I was in Italy playing for Scotland against Brazil, always a personal highlight for players to be in that particular company, and especially so during the World Cup finals.

The night became a blur for me, quite literally, when I absorbed the full impact of a free kick taken by Brazil's Branco and was knocked cold. In those days they called it concussion. Today's medical experts prefer to term it a brain trauma injury.

Regardless of the medical terminology that was most accurate, I was out like a light and was reputed to have asked my one-time Celtic and Scotland teammate, Roy Aitken, which way we were shooting once the game had resumed.

I have to tell you I don't know if that particular piece of folklore is true or false because, decades on, I still have no recollection of going to that game or returning back to the team's hotel afterwards.

What will now strike modern day students of cases like these as alarming is that I was allowed to continue playing after receiving treatment, and then collapsed in a heap a minute later. At which point I was taken to the dressing room and instructed not to let my eyes close. The same instruction was given to me when I was back in my bedroom at the hotel.

There was a time before medical studies started to produce disturbing figures, like players being three and a half times more likely to develop dementia than any other sector of society, when I would play along with all of the innocent banter surrounding my discomfort that night.

Innocent, because we didn't know any better at the time.

We were football players and not clinicians. Laymen and not medical experts.

Legend has it that Branco had earlier thundered a free kick at Scotland's defensive wall which had struck Mo Johnston on the thigh and caused him severe discomfort. When Brazil were awarded another free kick later on in the match, Ally McCoist had remembered the previous incident and asked me to swap places with him in our wall. Ally had clearly given the whole business a lot more thought than I had and so I let him trade places with me.

The rest is history. A history that is related to me through newspaper cuttings from the time and the anecdotal evidence of those who were there.

Ally, according to eyewitnesses, came into the dressing room at full-time and said, while looking in my direction, 'It could've been worse, wee man. It could've been me!'

An innocent jest once again and nothing to get upset about.

I stayed on in Italy after Scotland had been eliminated from the tournament and had a holiday there with my wife before returning to Borussia Dortmund for pre-season training.

The headaches I had suffered in Italy still persisted and three weeks into training I was sent to hospital for a brain scan. The examination showed there had been no lasting damage and, after a period of rest, I resumed my career. That meant eventually going on to play for Hibs and winning a cup final as well as helping Wim Jansen coach Celtic to a league title and then managing Partick Thistle and Dumbarton before my time in that side of the game was over and I moved into the media. In other words, a decade without after-effects relating to Branco and his free kick.

Remarkably, two decades after I'd played against Brazil, a letter was forwarded on to me by the Scottish Football Association. It had been sent by a journalist from Brazil who was engaged in writing Branco's autobiography following the player's retirement from the game. The communication was simple and straightforward. He wanted to know if I was alive or dead.

The free kick was, admittedly, the hardest blow to the head I had ever known as a player and what happened thereafter was, the German doctors told me, the equivalent of an aftershock. But I was very definitely alive and the letter actually brought a smile to my face.

I said one thing at the time which still holds true today. Some legendary figures in the game have never had the honour of playing for their country in a World Cup, but I have known that feeling and if the experience involved being knocked senseless then I take that as part of the deal.

My irony was that it would be heart problems, and not head injuries, which endangered my life on two occasions when I had given up playing the game.

But I can in no way minimise the extent of the problem that has robbed me, and their families, of people I loved in football.

None more so than Billy McNeill.

One of my regrets in life is that when a statue of Billy was unveiled in his birthplace of Bellshill I had only just come out of hospital. The ceremony was a matter of days after my discharge. It felt more like being released, after spending so much time on a ventilator following heart surgery that had come with life-threatening complications.

Billy's family had extended a personal invitation to me, but I just didn't have the physical strength at that time to make the journey from my home to Lanarkshire.

The big man had been so important in my life, being the one who took me to Celtic from Dumbarton and had gambled so much of the club's money on a twenty-year-old novice.

When people talked about Billy's own capabilities as a player, his heading of the ball was always prominent in the discussion. It didn't matter if teams used zonal marking or went man for man in the penalty box, Billy would either rise majestically to score a goal at one end or head the ball away and cancel out any threat if he was at the other end of the park.

What was one of the most iconic images of Big Billy?

It was the header that scored the goal which beat Dunfermline 3–2 in the Scottish Cup final of 1965 and gave Jock Stein his first trophy as Celtic manager. It could be said that that day marked the birth of the modern-day Celtic after eight years without a major trophy win. It was Billy who made that happen and I was lucky enough to have been involved in some of those treasured moments as one of his players.

When Billy's wife, Liz, broke the news to the country at large that he was suffering from dementia I wanted to see him. I took my grandson, Ross, with me because Billy was great with kids and the two of them hit it off straight away. I knew I was getting a response from the big man as well because he called me by my first name and that meant everything to me.

Billy passed away on 22 April 2019, but he is immortal in the eyes of the fans because he was Celtic.

Billy was a centre back and they carry the can when it comes to the consequences of heading the ball. They are the magnets attracted to the ball for their team's sake. Medical science is now dedicated to deciding what's best going forward when it comes to repetitive heading of the ball and the game needs to follow the guidelines laid down.

The loss of people like Billy and Stevie Chalmers, another Celtic legend taken before his time under the same circumstances, can't be allowed to pass without hoping that medical advances will spare others.

But, at the same time, I want to see everyone protected. Junior players and amateur players have lives that matter as well. My grandchildren play football and head the ball. The first thing parents do when they buy their children a ball is throw it to them at head height and look for it to be nodded back to them.

I don't think it is realistic to imagine that heading will be banned from the professional game altogether. How would Billy McNeill have felt as a player if his beloved Celtic were going to lose a game because of a ball going into the net at head height and he wasn't allowed to come to the rescue and deflect it away?

I want medicine and football to combine to life-saving effect while not endangering the game itself. And my support for the medical people is unquestioning. After all, I wouldn't be here today if it wasn't for medical science.

12

Riot, Burglary and Bank

IT WAS A BURGLARY at my home in the 1980s while I was with Celtic that taught me the true value of the medals I had won, and would go on to win, with the club. The lesson I learned one Saturday evening was that if you don't know the value of the prizes you have won as a player then you won't understand what anything is worth in the game.

I was going into our house in Helensburgh after a game at Celtic Park. The plan was for my wife and I to get our daughters settled, welcome in the babysitter, and then set off again to attend Tommy Burns' birthday party in Glasgow. But it was immediately obvious that all was not well.

Doors were lying wide open and we had clearly been the victim of unwanted intruders.

My wife's fears were based on a mother's sentimentality. Our older daughter, Gilan, had just celebrated her birthday and the monetary gifts she had been given by relatives were still in her bedroom. But once Mhairi was delighted to discover everything was where it should be there, an awful thought struck me. My medals were in our bedroom and by that time I had accumulated the full set of domestic honours with Celtic.

Thankfully, four league championship medals, two from the Scottish Cup and one League Cup final medal were still where I had left them.

But not for long.

First thing on the Monday morning, their next resting place was in a bank vault, to be joined by a fifth league medal at the end of the season. I realised I had got away with one where the burglary was concerned. The intruders had obviously been disturbed and scarpered without stealing treasured possessions that were invaluable to me.

Any inventory of a Celtic player's medals would place the ones won against Rangers at the top of the list for valuation. I've played in derby matches in three cities – Glasgow, Dortmund and Edinburgh – and there is absolutely nothing that comes near to the intensity of Celtic versus Rangers.

When I was with Hibs in the latter stages of my career, we were part of a derby with Hearts which divided a city.

When I was at Borussia Dortmund before then and we were playing Schalke, it was a derby which divided the North Rhine-Westphalia region of Germany.

But when I was with Celtic, and we were playing Rangers, it was a derby that divided an entire country.

You understand these things when you're at Celtic Park and the club tells you they have a request from a supporters' club in Elgin to have you visit them for a function after a game on a Saturday night.

I went to loads of those events, and did so happily because I knew I was popular with the Celtic fans and I also understood exactly why that was the case. I had that happiest of all happy knacks for a Celtic player. I scored regularly against Rangers or else I was a serial winner against them in cup finals.

Those goals, like the one that won the league and left Rangers second in the table in 1979 and then the League Cup final winner against them in 1982 at Hampden, cemented my popularity. In between, there was the Scottish Cup final win in 1980 for Billy McNeill over John Greig's Rangers that will never be forgotten for a variety of reasons.

It was the final that provoked a full-scale riot and introduced government legislation that took alcohol out of Scotland's football grounds under the terms of the Criminal Justice (Scotland) Act. Legislation which remains on the statute books to this day.

I had only ever been to one game between Celtic and Rangers before I got to play in my first derby in 1978. I was still at primary school and the father of a classmate took the pair of us to a game at Celtic Park. I remember being taken aback by the noise and the drama of the occasion, but then a Rangers player was sent off and the atmosphere changed to something more intimidating.

Those were the days when any fan old enough to buy alcohol could still take a carry-out into any ground unchallenged. And you could have as much to drink as you fancied.

All of a sudden, beer bottles started to rain down and a coat was placed over the heads of two wee boys to offer what protection it could from the possibility of serious injury. I was scared stiff.

And so was my wife as she sat terrified in the main stand at Hampden and watched carnage unfold after

Celtic had beaten Rangers in the Scottish Cup final after extra time.

It was barely believable mayhem on a scale that prompted government legislation, even though the players were only truly aware of what had happened when we saw it on television afterwards.

Clear directives are given to the Celtic and Rangers players by the police before an occasion like that in the interests of maintaining public order.

At Celtic Park, we were told that, if we won the cup, the players would be allowed to take the trophy to those parts of the ground where our fans were congregated after the official presentation on the winners rostrum.

And that's what we did, before going up the tunnel for what were lavish celebrations in our dressing room.

I had been with the BBC as a pundit for a time after my playing days ended, being there at the same time as the highly respected match commentator, Archie Macpherson. There can't be anyone who was old enough to remember the Scottish Cup final at Hampden in 1980 who doesn't recall Archie's description of what was unfolding in front of him.

'It's like a scene from *Apocalypse Now*,' he said during the live television presentation.

I only know that because the moment has been replayed so many times since then. On the day, I was entirely unaware that fans were coming over a ten-foot-high perimeter fence to get onto the pitch.

The very thought of a ten-foot-high fence is incredible now. It would be unthinkable that such a thing could be erected inside a football ground today.

It might also now be time to re-examine the alcohol ban on supporters while we're at it. When I was playing in the Bundesliga, crowds the length and breadth of Germany could have beers in plastic cups during games and there was never any bother. When you think about it, the fans in Scotland today are being punished for the sins of people who are now old enough to be grandfathers.

I remember we went to the Grosvenor Hotel in Glasgow's West End with our wives and partners after that game at Hampden and Big Billy gave a short, but dignified speech on the events of what had been a controversial day to say the least.

Billy was a born leader of men and so was our captain that afternoon, Danny McGrain. Danny was heavily involved in the goal that won the cup and he was, in my estimation, a world-class full back. In his time, he had overcome a fractured skull and diabetes by showing the strong mentality that was his dominant characteristic. He was, is, and will forever be a club legend who gave his teammates a strong sense of reassurance just to know he was there beside us.

Danny also detested losing matches and he wasn't slow to let you know how much it hurt if a defeat was suffered.

The cup final had been deep into extra-time after a goalless ninety minutes against Rangers when Danny, who normally had to be dragged into the opposition's half of the field, appeared across the halfway line with thirteen minutes to go. He must have used a 1980s prototype satnav to get there!

Even more surprising than the geography of the situation was the fact Danny had a shot at goal which had Rangers' goalkeeper, Peter McCloy, going one way before

George McCluskey deflected the ball in the opposite direction and won the cup. It was an astonishing and iconic moment.

There are some Celtic players the Rangers fans would have loved to have seen in their team. Every decade produces them. Danny McGrain was definitely one of them and Kenny Dalglish would have been another. I must be eligible for entry to that elite group, if only for the reason that I've lost count of the number of Rangers supporters who have told me over the years that I was a good player who had made the mistake of signing for the wrong club.

I turned down two approaches to go to Rangers and I have no regrets at all about any decision taken because I went to the right club for me.

And you need to have the courage of your convictions when you reject Jock Wallace while you're still at school and John Greig when there's a statue of the man outside Ibrox.

There were others on our side, of course, who revelled in noising up the Rangers fans. On the day we won the cup in 1980 we had guys in our team like big Roy Aitken, Tommy Burns, George McCluskey, Frank McGarvey and most certainly Johnny Doyle, who were steeped in the club and had an intimate understanding of the rivalry with Rangers. And they made their pleasure highly visible, and audible, whenever we beat them.

If that victory happened to be at Ibrox then the decibel level was always that bit louder when the songs of victory were being sung in the away dressing room. The smile on your face as you walked out the front door at Ibrox to board the team bus was always broader than normal into the bargain while you were getting dogs abuse from the Rangers fans.

I always felt my style of play was made for the Celtic–Rangers game and maybe that's why I enjoyed them so much and had a satisfactory degree of success in them. I know there would have been something missing from my professional life if I had never experienced the peculiar sensation of playing in that unique derby.

I just had to remember to be careful where I put the winners medals, that's all.

13

I Would Walk 500 Miles

ON THE MOST FAMOUS DATE in Celtic's history, 25 May, I made my full international debut for Scotland. And the manager who ingrained that date on the minds of the Celtic supporters when the European Cup was won against Inter Milan in Lisbon, the legendary Jock Stein, was the man who made a dream come true for me.

The year was 1985 and England provided the opposition at Hampden in what was known as the Rous Cup, a short-lived friendly competition with a ceremonial trophy at stake. The match was a device to keep the Scotland versus England fixture on an annual basis after the discontinuation of what was known as the Home International Championships the year before.

But crowd trouble crept into the fixture in the streets away from Hampden or Wembley and the English FA took fright because their clubs were already banned from European competition due to an upsurge in fan disorder at that time. They feared further action might be taken against them and so the competition was abandoned in 1989.

But on 25 May 1985 I came off the subs bench, to replace Gordon Strachan no less, and play the final twenty minutes of a game won by Scotland due to a single goal scored by Richard Gough with a header.

The occasion marked a highlight in my career, of course, even if it had taken me a while to get there.

Talk about I would walk five hundred miles and I would walk five hundred more. It had felt like a marathon journey to reach that personal milestone.

I'd been in Celtic's first team for six years and I had won all there was to win at a domestic level in Scotland, but recognition on the international front was a long time coming and a relatively short-lived experience into the bargain.

Twenty caps in total. One goal scored in a friendly match against Chile. And that was that for me.

But I treasure every moment I played for my country and I had no fight to pick with anyone over the time it took me to realise my lifelong ambition.

The story of how I eventually got there in front of 66,000 people, much more than could get into the national stadium today, was stranger than fiction. I thought I was good enough to play for Scotland, but every time a squad was announced on the radio sports bulletins my name was missing.

And then Neilly Mochan, the Celtic kit-man who had known Mr Stein since they played in the same team together and recorded a record-breaking 7–1 win over Rangers in the League Cup final in 1957, put me in the picture over why I was out of the reckoning.

The West of Scotland based radio station, Radio Clyde, had a massively popular pundit at the time by the name of James Sanderson. Listeners hung on his every word, and he was a giant of Scottish broadcasting.

My problem was that Big Jock wasn't going to put in any player, whether he played for Celtic or anybody else, because a pundit had said it had to happen.

'When wee Jimmy goes, you'll get into the team,' Neilly said to me, with deadly accuracy.

James gave up his radio work at the beginning of 1985 to work for the Commonwealth Games organisers in Edinburgh and the persistent call for MacLeod to be picked for Scotland went with him.

Neilly had sat beside Jock on Celtic's bench for enough years to know that the only thing which activated his mind during a match was the pull of his own instincts. And that had been good enough to land Celtic the most prestigious European trophy and become the first club in Scottish football history to win nine league titles in a row. It was a characteristic used during domestic matches with no negative side effects.

Neilly said if the crowd at Celtic Park chanted the name of one of the subs in the hope of changing the manager's mind, he would turn to the player being singled out and tell him he would be as well going up the tunnel and sitting in the home dressing room.

But when the phone rang, and I heard the voice, I was still unsure enough of myself to wonder if it was my Celtic teammate, Roy Aitken, playing an elaborate trick on me. Roy was a first-class impressionist, and his Jock Stein voice was good enough to fool anyone.

But the call from Mr Stein was one hundred per cent authentic. It was what he had to say which threw me. Jock was asking if I'd turn out as an over-age player in Scotland's Under-21 team to face Iceland in Reykjavik. I didn't take that as a slight on my reputation. I accepted straight away, only to have him back on the phone half an hour later to see if I'd be agreeable to forgetting about the original idea and playing against England for the full international team instead.

I'd never had the opportunity to speak to the great man before those two telephone calls in one day, but it wasn't long before we were speaking again and I got the rough edge of his tongue.

The squad to face England gathered at the Gleneagles Hotel and I was told to room with Jim Bett, who had played for Aberdeen and Rangers. We were given a form to fill in for dinner and against the word 'Starter' I had put down prawn cocktail.

When it came time for dinner to be served, Jock spotted the unwise choice I had made.

'Who ordered the prawn cocktail?' he said.

When I admitted it had been me his next question was, 'Do you have prawn cocktail in the house on a Friday night?'

I had to admit it was not part of the MacLeod family's staple diet and Jock finished the question-and-answer session abruptly by saying it wasn't on his list of dietary requirements in that case.

The following day our next exchange had my heart pounding for a different reason. There were twenty minutes to go when he called me towards him and told me to get on the park and play on the left-hand side of midfield.

My dream then had a time and date, as well as a position on the park and a happy ending. You never forget the first manager to give you a cap.

Tragically, the next overwhelming memory I have of Jock is being with the Scotland squad when we beat Wales in Cardiff to qualify for the 1986 World Cup finals. I was standing in the tunnel after Davie Cooper had decided the game with a penalty for us and I watched tragedy unfold.

Jock collapsed on the touchline having suffered a heart attack and he was on a stretcher by the time he went past Arthur and me to be worked on by the medical people.

We then walked into the oddest dressing room I had ever known.

Scotland had qualified for the World Cup finals in Argentina and you could have heard a pin drop. Nobody spoke and the scenes of distress were only too evident.

On a club level, the greatest manager Celtic had ever known was gone and the sense of loss was incalculable.

I only had a short time under his wing but he impressed me as much as any other person in our game. You listened to him and you followed his instructions on the park.

It's a huge understatement to say that Jock Stein was a hard act to follow as Scotland manager. But it was a job that had to be done and the man to get it was Andy Roxburgh.

I liked Andy, particularly as he always had faith in me as a player. That gave me the confidence to go out and do the job he asked of me on the park and try to produce my best form for my country.

Everyone's heard the stories about players being brought together for games of Trivial Pursuit and some putting that down as a black mark against Andy's man-management methods. But what's wrong with that?

I always tried my damnedest to win because I was competitive by nature and every time Andy gave me another full cap it was the best feeling in the world for me.

Twenty caps in total might not seem like a lot but when you consider that Jimmy Johnstone, voted the best-ever player in Celtic's history by the fans, only got three more than that, then it doesn't look so bad. Other than to wonder how somebody as good as Jimmy could end up with such a meagre number against their name when he was also inducted into Scottish Football's Hall of Fame in 2004.

After his passing, the wee man even tried to guide me towards a fortune in a casino in Australia one afternoon when ex-players had been to a Celtic supporters convention. Jimmy's wife, Agnes, accompanied my wife and me everywhere on that trip, from an Osmonds concert to the roulette wheel.

I saw Agnes walking towards me in the casino and decided to put my profit for the day on number seven, to honour Jinky's memory. But, in a gesture that must have had Jimmy doing his celestial nut, I changed my mind and went for number 11 instead. I don't think I need to tell you what happened next.

Mhairi and I shared the same wedding anniversary date as Agnes and Jimmy, 11 June, and when we got home to Scotland there was a card congratulating us and inside it one hundred pounds in cash.

We attempted to protest and turn down her generosity but Agnes simply said, 'If you return it to me, I'll just send it straight back to you by return of post.' You have the good fortune to meet special people in this game and Agnes is certainly one of them.

★

I wanted more caps for Scotland than the twenty in total that came my way, but that's not the same as saying I thought I was entitled to more than that number.

When I was a teenager playing for Dumbarton in the lower leagues and desperate to make my way in the game, I went to Hampden one evening to see Scotland. There wasn't a ball in sight and there was no opposing team anywhere about, either. I was a kid who, like the thousands of other people I had for company inside the ground, had bought into the national hysteria surrounding the team who had qualified for the World Cup finals in Argentina in 1978.

Ally MacLeod was the manager at that time and he had charisma to spare, enough to bring people to Hampden in their droves to wave off the team as they left for South America. If you had told me that night I would play for my country at full international level on twenty occasions I would have bitten your hand off to make that statement come true. Even though the trip to Argentina would bear all of the traditional hallmarks of the national team – a doping scandal, a narrow failure to get out of our group, while still contriving, through Archie Gemmill, to score the Goal of the Tournament against Holland, before we came back home again a lot earlier than Ally had promised. Without winning the World Cup.

★

It wasn't as if I was going to say to Mr Stein, 'What took you so long to pick me in the first place?' Or ask him and his successor, Andy Roxburgh, why they didn't pick me more often. I know for sure that the conversation with the former would have been considerably shorter than the one I might have had with the latter.

In truth, I played in an era when Scotland was spoiled for choice when it came to playing talent. For example, my teammates on the bench at Hampden when I made my international debut were Mo Johnston, Maurice Malpas, Paul McStay and Alan Rough. What must the starting eleven have been like if the guys sitting beside me were the stand-bys?

The one time I swapped a Scotland shirt for an England jersey also proved the wealth of talent there was in Britain at that time before the influx of foreign players that would follow years later. I was told before the game that Chris Waddle was one-footed and the other one was just for standing on so far as he was concerned. Nothing could have been further from the truth, as I discovered when I put that theory to the test on the park.

We exchanged jerseys as a mark of mutual respect afterwards, which got me out of a row with my Celtic teammate, big Roy Aitken. I had remembered Roy haranguing another Celtic player, who shall remain nameless, for asking an opposing player for his top at the end of a European tie. The big man was wholeheartedly against the idea of running after someone for their top as a souvenir. It was a different matter if two players had enjoyed their contest against one another and exchanged shirts as a memento of that occasion.

I noticed a couple of Scotland players go after Kylian Mbappé to ask for his jersey the last time we played France in a friendly match in Lille. I don't know if they ever got it, but I have to tell you I do have his shirt, autographed into the bargain, in my house. And, fortunately, I didn't even have to chase him about for ninety minutes on the park to get that much sought-after strip. I just sat in the foyer of a hotel in Paris and the manager brought one to me as a present.

GOALS AGAINST RANGERS became my speciality with Celtic. This shot made it four-all in an epic derby at Ibrox.

THAT WINNING FEELING. How could you lose with guys like Tommy Burns, Danny McGrain and Roy Aitken in your team?

I ASSOCIATE WITH THE SONG WHICH SAYS the higher you build your barriers the taller I become.

I NEVER THOUGHT REFEREES WERE BIASED against Celtic, but that didn't stop me from arguing with them.

THE NIGHT I PLAYED for Borussia Dortmund against Celtic in Glasgow, I got an ovation that will live with me forever.

AFTER LOSING ALL OF MY TOES I went back to Celtic Park with my grandson, Fergus. Both of us were on our own two feet.

WE'RE IN HIS HEART, we're in his soul. Sir Rod Stewart loves watching Celtic and it was a pleasure for Mhairi, young Mhairi and Fergus, along with myself, to meet him in the boardroom.

WALKING IN A JANSEN WONDERLAND. We stopped Rangers from winning Ten in a Row and the Celtic fans will never forget that.

WIM TOLD ME TO SIT DOWN and stop ranting at the players when we had our first friendly match. Check the pained expression on his face.

A LEAGUE AND LEAGUE CUP DOUBLE was a magnificent return for one season together.

THE TEAM THAT STICKS TOGETHER, wins together. Mhairi and me with Wim and his wife, Coby.

THE YOUNG ONES. I used all my best chat up lines to get a date with this girl.

THE CHAT UP LINES were a success. The girl and I got married.

THE BEST CONTRACT I ever signed was the marriage contract.

IN THE BRIDAL CAR on the way to a new way of life.

THIS LOT REFUSED to let me go when the doctors said there was no hope and sang me back to life.

THE FIRST TEAM. Gilan, Mhairi, me, young Mhairi and Marina. Parents and daughters.

MY COACHING LIFE began at Hibs with Alex Miller when I came home from Germany. The League Cup win showed we were successful together.

MANAGING PARTICK THISTLE ended sadly because of a referee – someone I have never spoken to since the decision he took sunk my team. Marina is my babe in arms.

MANAGED DUMBARTON to promotion and earned my place in the club's Hall of Fame.

I WOULD HAVE GLADLY had these two up front for me in the managerial days. John Hartson and Frank McAvennie were good on the golf course too.

GOLF WAS MY RELAXATION. I look forward to another round with Archie Macpherson one day.

TWENTY CAPS FOR SCOTLAND meant the world to me, even the night I was knocked out cold in Italy.

JOCK STEIN WAS RELUCTANT to pick me for a reason. Andy Roxburgh had no worries about putting me in his Scotland team.

The Ryder Cup golf tournament was being played in France in 2017 and, golf nut as I am, I had gone there with a friend, Fergus Stewart, who worked in the hotel industry. When our hotel manager recognised me as the man who had once played for Celtic and Borussia Dortmund, he went off to present us with a couple of gifts he had packed away to mark the occasion when we were his paying guests.

First of all he presented Fergus with the Paris Saint-Germain jersey worn by Neymar, and then he gave me Mbappé's signed shirt for posterity.

When I got home there was exasperation over the fact I hadn't got Neymar's top and questions were raised over who this guy Mbappé was to begin with and what did he amount to in the game?

Years later Mbappé was the name on everyone's lips, and I have often thought about the moment I got my hands on his jersey while watching him become one of the best players in the world.

You just never know is the phrase which covers moments like that. Unless you take another route to see if you can find out what the future might hold for you.

My sister-in-law was a hairdresser and one of her clients happened to be a clairvoyant, fortune teller, call her what you will. The general consensus of opinion was that, whatever you called her, Helen Cochrane knew her stuff. I don't know whether it has to do with my father coming from the Highlands or not, but I have always been fascinated by that kind of thing.

So, I made an appointment to see Helen while I was still a Celtic player and she told me I would wear black and yellow, but also blue, at my next club and would stay with them for three years.

Dortmund wore black and yellow, of course, and the training tops we put on each day were blue. And she was as good as her word with the bit about staying in Germany for three years.

She even told me I would go to work at two different grounds and that was when I began to doubt her ability to see into the future.

Until I got to Dortmund and understood that, while we played our home games at what was then the West-falenstadion, we trained each day at a ground known as the Rote Erde.

Helen was bang on.

In Scotland we say, 'What's for you won't go by you.'

I got my Scotland caps in the end and I took great satis-faction from winning every one of them. I wanted more, but it was not to be.

I got to play for my country against Brazil, the best of the best, at the World Cup finals, even if people only want to talk about a free kick in that game and how painful the moment must have been for me when I was knocked unconscious by it.

That night in Italy was the fulfilment of a lifetime ambi-tion for the kid who went to see Scotland when there was no game to see and had dreams about one day wearing my country's jersey. How can you feel hard done by after an experience like that?

It was worth the pain.

★

My final association with the Scotland national team came in the World Cup finals in France in 1998. I was working for the SFA, compiling reports on Scotland's opponents, giving them to Andy and his assistant, Craig Brown.

As mentioned earlier, the day before we flew out to France, Craig's brother, Jock, had told me my time was up at Celtic, despite assisting Wim Jansen when we stopped Rangers winning Ten in a Row. We agreed to draw a veil over the whole business and focus on the job at hand.

Qualifying for big international tournaments is never easy and it was a privilege to both play in them and to assist the coaching staff in 1998. Playing any part in that for your country is an honour. So why haven't Scotland qualified for the World Cup finals since 1998? We've had six attempts since then and six failures. Why?

I'm tempted to say you can search me for an answer. But I'll float one idea, and that is we need another Roy Aitken. What a driving force he was. Quick. Strong. Fearless. And blessed with the great attitude he had shown since making his debut for Celtic at the age of sixteen.

And I'm glad it wasn't him imitating Jock Stein on the phone that day when the door to the Scotland dressing room was thrown open to welcome me in.

14

The Other Green and White

I LIKE TO THINK I PLAYED a large part in keeping Paul McStay at Celtic Park for five years longer than he might otherwise have stayed there, triggering a chain of events which ultimately led to Rangers being prevented from getting ten league titles in a row.

Nicknamed 'The Maestro', Paul McStay's name is an integral part of Celtic folklore and the family surname is woven deep into the fabric of the club through the contribution of earlier generations. But you can't have a lifetime attachment to a club as a player without there being ups and downs and episodes that cut deep into the soul because you care so much about who you represent.

On 2 May 1992, I played for Hibs against Celtic in Glasgow. I had left Borussia Dortmund for Edinburgh the year before and six months earlier Hibs had beaten Dunfermline to win the League Cup after overcoming Rangers at Hampden in the semi-finals.

Our decent run was matched only by the troubled times that engulfed my old team in the East End of Glasgow. Rangers were in the midst of the run that would take them to nine successive league championships.

Celtic had embarked on a difficult course involving managerial change on a regular basis and Fergus McCann was still two years away from revolutionising the football club he'd supported in his youth before he emigrated to North America.

On the day I encountered Paul and gave him the benefit of my experience, Celtic needed to take a point from Hibs at home in order to qualify for the following season's UEFA Cup on the basis of their league position.

It was probably indicative of the way their luck was going then that the match was less than ten minutes old when Derek Whyte scored an own goal. Pat McGinlay, who would later go on to play for Celtic, put Hibs further in front midway through the second half and Stevie Fulton got a consolation goal for Celtic in the last minute.

It was always a strange sensation for me to be on the winning side against Celtic, and I had done it before with Hibs on a domestic basis and with Borussia Dortmund in European competition.

My confused state of mind was nothing compared to the sadness I saw etched on Paul's face when I approached him at time-up to shake his hand. He told me he thought he had played his last match for Celtic because a lot of interest was being shown in him, particularly from abroad, and the thought of walking off the park for the final time was clearly making him highly emotional.

I felt I had to intervene, and I did.

I told Paul if he truly believed he wouldn't play in front of the Jungle again while wearing green and white hoops then he should turn around, run towards the fans and make some kind of gesture which showed how much he thought of their support. And if he hadn't entirely made up his mind to go elsewhere then he should go to them in any case and still let them know how much they, and the club, meant to him.

Either way, I told him, you'll regret it for the rest of your life if you do nothing at all and the moment passes.

I walked away, and when I looked back over my shoulder seconds later, I saw Paul throwing his jersey into the crowd. The gesture was widely interpreted by all who witnessed it as the moment Paul said goodbye to Celtic.

What was supposed to be a tear-stained farewell turned out instead to be the pivotal moment that saw Paul re-evaluate where he stood at Celtic. He stayed on and, three years later, captained the team to a Scottish Cup final win over Airdrie that would give him the moment of victory he cherished. It was also the day Tommy Burns got the managerial accolade his time in charge at Celtic so richly merited.

Not only did I get the satisfaction of knowing I had been there when the course of history was altered for one man, I would then join up with Wim Jansen to form the managerial team who ultimately stopped Rangers' title-winning run at nine in a row. And Paul McStay was in that squad.

Of course, I couldn't possibly have foreseen all of that taking place when I rejected Dortmund's offer of a contract extension and returned home to Scotland from Germany. I knew I had plenty of football left in me and I wasn't content to be a bit-part player in the Bundesliga because of the political constraints caused by the newly adopted Three Foreigner Rule.

I could have signed for Dunfermline, and they were a terrific club to deal with, but they saw me as a player and nothing else. Hibs, who were then managed by Alex Miller, wanted me to go to Easter Road as his assistant and that was more to my liking in terms of future planning.

I would never Billy Big-time anyone in football. I was perfectly happy trading the Bundesliga for a return to what was then called the Scottish League and I had a feeling my trophy-winning days weren't at an end either.

I felt the same when I left Celtic for Dortmund in 1987 and I was proved correct when we beat Werder Bremen in the German Cup final in Berlin a year later. It was the first trophy Borussia had won since 1965, a remarkable statistic when you think of how it all turned out to be for them in later years under Jürgen Klopp.

Hibs had been without a win in the Scottish Cup final since 1902, nearly ninety years earlier, and it had been twenty-six years since they lifted the League Cup. But I had the oddest feeling I was on a roll.

I gave Hibs my heart and soul.

The travelling was too great for me from Helensburgh to Edinburgh and back every day for training, so I uprooted my family and we moved to the east side of the country. I immersed myself in the club and got to know the fans.

I had this intuitive feeling that we were going to win the League Cup in 1991 and I told every supporter they should have a punt on us to do just that.

No one employed by a senior football club can have a bet on the games they play in and that's a rule as old as I am. It's seen as a temptation leading to unlawful and unwanted betting patterns and the game is also strewn with professional players whose lives have got into difficulty due to gambling addiction.

I fully accept, and understand, all of that. But the game of football has commercial relations with betting companies and if the people who support those clubs wish to gamble responsibly on football competitions, then it's their disposable income and their prerogative.

We started by knocking out Stirling Albion and then followed that up by eliminating both halves of Ayrshire; Kilmarnock and Ayr United. The ultimate test of my theory that Hibs and the League Cup were magnetically attracted to each other came when we drew Rangers at Hampden in the semi-finals.

My thinking was that it was best to get them at the penultimate stage of the tournament rather than the final, when tension and concentration tends to be higher for the team inevitably cast as the favourites to win.

My instincts were correct. Andy Goram made an uncharacteristic mistake in goal for Rangers and our striker, Keith Wright, pounced to score the only goal of the game.

The team I could have joined instead of Hibs, Dunfermline, were our opponents in the final. A side containing big Davie Moyes, no less, but we were too much for them on the day and another goal from Keith, along with one from Tommy McIntyre, took the cup to Easter Road.

I met one fan afterwards who had always told me he'd followed my advice in fancying Hibs for the cup win and had a wager on us before a ball was kicked for real. When I asked him what the bookmaker had said when he eventually collected his winnings, he told me his words were, 'Don't f**king come back.'

To achieve is what you are there to do in football if you're a professional. That was my intention when I signed for

Hibs and that was my reason for leaving the club when my contract ended. The manager wanted me to hang up my boots and concentrate on coaching to the exclusion of all else. But I had this nagging doubt at the back of my mind that the old legs still had strength enough to carry me a bit further yet, so I went back to where it had all started for me in the game. Dumbarton.

This will sound bizarre bordering on the nonsensical, but what I did there gave me a memory that comes third in my list of greatest moments after joining up with Wim and stopping Rangers from winning Ten in a Row.

One event took place in front of tens of thousands of jubilant fans moved to tears and swept along on a tidal wave of emotion. The other one took place at Forthbank Stadium, the home of Stirling Albion.

It was the last day of the season in 1995 and we needed a win to seal promotion from the bottom tier of Scottish football. The game was goalless at half-time and, as I tried to settle my team in the away dressing room, I could hear someone in the one next door screaming, 'They're beat. They're done.'

I went off on one immediately, asking my players if they could hear the way they were being disrespected and dismissed and telling them that had to be their motivation for proving they were nowhere near down and out.

I put myself back out for the second half and played the full ninety minutes while the adrenaline pumped through my body. We scored twice and went up. I went to embrace my family and the Dumbarton fans. I didn't want the good of the day to be marred by any form of altercation. What was said about us being a spent force was premature and uncalled for. It was also a self-defeating tactic because it gave Dumbarton the impetus to ram the words down the opposition's throats. The motivation had served us well.

We had endured. We had achieved. And it was a very sweet moment indeed.

I still have my certificate from the night I was inducted into Dumbarton's Hall of Fame on the back of moments like that and getting the club a six-figure cheque from Celtic to begin my time in the game's top flight. Going back to Dumbarton was absolutely the right decision for me and it's one I have never, ever regretted.

15

Pat McGinlay on Murdo

I WAS BORN FIVE DAYS AFTER CELTIC WON the European Cup by beating Inter Milan in Lisbon in 1967. Celtic was my team from childhood and I was on a supporters' bus going to games from my home in Partick as soon as I was old enough to become an excited passenger.

Murdo MacLeod was my hero when I stood in the old Jungle at Celtic Park. They say you should never meet your heroes because it can often result in disappointment due to the image you had of them being tarnished by regrettable experience. In this case, I met my hero, I played beside him as a Hibs player and I was captained by him when we beat Dunfermline to win the League Cup final in 1991. And at no stage was there the slightest possibility that the high esteem in which I had always held Murdo was going to be diminished. It only grew in an ever-increasing way because of the person, and the professional, I found him to be.

When you're a young player at Easter Road, as I was when the news broke, and you hear that Murdo MacLeod is going to leave Borussia Dortmund in the Bundesliga and sign for Hibs, it was only natural to wonder how he would respond to the move back to Scotland.

Would it be the equivalent of topping up his pension fund? Would he swan about the place while acting as if he was doing all of us a favour by having him in our midst? He had won all there was to win on a domestic basis when he was at Celtic, and he had been a major part of a Dortmund team who had won the German Cup during his stay there. In other words, were his motives self-indulgent, or was he self-assured enough to know that he still had plenty to offer the game?

I got my answer on the very first day he walked into the dressing room and overwhelmed me with his strength of character and ingrained professionalism. He wasn't there to do any of us a favour. He was there to make me, and the rest, raise our game to his own impeccably high standards.

Murdo wasn't running down any clock. He was winding us up to reach new heights of endeavour through leading by example. I knew after our first training session that he was making demands of us rather than the other way round. Murdo was flying into tackles and getting about the pitch like I remembered him doing every week at Celtic Park.

He took me under his wing and I felt I was being fast-tracked in the game by a man who was giving me the benefit of his considerable experience.

Murdo obviously knew of no other way to conduct himself. He played in training games the same way he approached league matches on a Saturday, and all the while I knew I was sharing a dressing room with a thoroughly decent, down-to-earth person.

There was only one moment when he took me by surprise, and that was the day he drove into the ground

128

with his new car, a Mercedes 500 convertible. Heated seats, the works. My wife and kids had become firm friends with Murdo and his family by that stage and he gave the children a spin along the bypass in Edinburgh one day to let them enjoy the wow factor.

It was Murdo's wife, Mhairi, who rationalised that particular purchase by pointing out that Murdo had earned his money by his own hard work and commitment over a fair number of years. If he wanted to buy an expensive car, that was his prerogative. And I wasn't about to argue with that when I knew I was getting free tuition on how to be a better football player on a daily basis from the man behind the wheel.

There was an aura about him and that was never better exemplified than on the day we won the League Cup. Our run to Hampden didn't start in the most glamorous fashion. We played Stirling Albion at the neutral venue of St Johnstone's ground because their own pitch had an artificial surface and, in those days, you could opt out on the basis they would have had an unfair advantage over you. After our win there, Murdo told us he really and truly believed we had the depth of talent to win the competition.

That belief sustained us through subsequent wins against Kilmarnock and Ayr United, but then we were drawn against Rangers, the holders of the trophy, in the semi-final at Hampden. The normal equation is that playing Celtic or Rangers in Glasgow made the opposition the underdogs by tradition and painful experience.

Our manager, Alex Miller, was impeccable in his preparation and tactical knowledge. That was a given.

Our captain, Murdo, was an inspirational people person. He knew how much it meant to him, and a Celtic supporter like me, to beat Rangers against all the odds, and a solitary goal from Keith Wright, who scored in every round of the competition, including the final, won the game for us.

It was such an unbelievable feeling for me and I was still on a high when I decided to take my wife, Margaret, for a celebratory drink before we went home. We went to the Beechwood Hotel, a short walk from Hampden, and it was the security men on the door who brought me back down to earth by pointing out that the bar was full of Rangers supporters, and I might not be their idea of a suitable drinking companion.

The penultimate stage was one thing. The day of the final itself was the real eye opener. We were the favourites to beat Dunfermline but Murdo detested complacency, or the very idea of it, and so he came into the dressing room like a man ready to take a flamethrower to the place.

His first words were, 'This is our effing day.'

He was going round every player, physically grabbing some of us in the process to underline the seriousness of his intent, and using more industrial language to get across the message to us that defeat was simply not an acceptable option.

Murdo was essentially asking us what we had to give for the team on the day.

There's a way that top players walk, talk and carry themselves. They know how good they are and they don't need you letting them down because you can't aspire to those heights. It might be a cliché, but it is true, nevertheless. That kind of thing is infectious. You would do anything not to let down this giant presence by your side in the tunnel as you wait to take the field.

By the time the game against Dunfermline got underway, I was absolutely convinced in my own mind that Hibs would win. And Keith Wright and Tommy McIntyre scored the goals that ensured we took the cup back to Edinburgh.

And we were all about to understand first-hand what it meant to Murdo.

There is a traditional cup final moment when the victorious team goes upstairs to the winners' podium. The captain is handed the trophy, holds it aloft to receive the acclaim of the fans, and then passes it down the line for the other players to do the same. Murdo accepted the cup, held it up, and then walked off the other side of the podium and down the stairs towards the pitch with the trophy under his arm.

This man who had won major prizes in two countries was so wrapped up in the moment of triumph he temporarily forgot what he was doing. It showed me that Murdo was savouring this cup win as much as he had done any other throughout his career. The fact it was Hibs didn't mean it was any less important than Celtic or Dortmund.

I respected all of that, but I still dig him up about leaving the rest of us standing there empty-handed every chance I get.

It was a dream and a privilege for me to play beside someone I had idolised when he was a player at Celtic Park and to understand that he was a humble man into the bargain. They say there are no real friendships in football, but I know that's not the case because I met someone who was a major, and lasting, influence on my life. I had a friend who made me more professional and raised my game to the extent I would eventually go on to play for Celtic and know the sensation of wearing that jersey.

Your playing career feels like it's over in a flash but there are times within it that stay with you forever. Playing beside Murdo and being his fellow cup winner will always live with me.

16

Genius and Tragedy

TOUCHED BY GENIUS. Tormented by tragedy.

That's how I look back on the Celtic side I was part of between 1980 and 1985.

We won the league title in 1982. The Scottish Cup in 1980 and 1985 and the League Cup final against Rangers in 1983, when I had the good fortune to score one of the best goals I ever managed to get in that derby.

It was a shot so sweetly struck that only the back of the net at Hampden prevented the ball from leaving the stadium, even if I say so myself.

I was part of a gang at Celtic Park. A reputable gang. We entertained our supporters and we had this reputation for retrieving apparently lost causes on the pitch while lifting people out of their seats as we did so.

And we did it on double egg and chips.

There was a café across from our training ground, next to the Celtic Supporters Social Club at Barrowfield. That was our meeting place after work, and double egg and chips was the plat du jour for the most part.

Today's nutritionists and diet co-ordinators at Lennoxtown might be astounded to know of our eating regime back then but it did us no harm out on the park in those more innocent, less sophisticated times.

It was also a privilege to share a dressing room, or a café table, with such a tight-knit group of players who were dedicated to achieving success for the club. You can't hope to be successful unless you have that bond and the unity of purpose to get you through the difficult times. We formed friendships for life and I only understood the accuracy of that statement when those lives were ended, threatened or disrupted in a severely damaging way.

From our nucleus of consistent performers, we had the horrific experience of losing Johnny Doyle to an accident at home in October 1981. Tragically, while still a Celtic player, he was electrocuted.

Tommy Burns, player, manager and icon at Celtic Park would have his life cut sadly short by cancer in 2008, prompting an outpouring of grief within the Celtic family which persists to this day, as anyone who has seen the stage production of his life story will readily testify.

Davie Provan was cut down in his prime at Celtic by the debilitating illness, ME, which terminated a glowing career that still had so much to give.

I myself have confronted death on two separate occasions, in 2010 and 2022, due to heart trouble and was mercifully spared to carry on with my life. And it was while recovering from the second of those confrontations with my own mortality that I encountered the greatest act of selfless courage I have ever known.

The door of room 210 in Ward C of the Golden Jubilee Hospital opened one day and in walked Frank McGarvey, another of the band of brothers from those days in the early 1980s. A visit from an old teammate would have been thought nothing remarkable, until the circumstances of that appearance at my bedside are recalled.

Days earlier, Frank had been diagnosed with pancreatic cancer and given the stark warning that he was dealing with a life-or-death situation. Somehow, under those devastating circumstances for him and his family, Frank's first thought had been to make a journey to my side and see how I was after coming off a ventilator that had been doing my breathing for me.

I don't mind admitting tears were shed as two frail bodies embraced and reminisced about the time when we had the world at our feet and the strength to do something about it. I felt humbled that someone who was embarking on his own battle for survival should think of another person before himself. But that was how we were in the dressing room that Frank joined from Liverpool in 1980 and became involved in what we'll call a turf war.

Celtic blood coursed through Frank's veins, and had done so every day since childhood. Doyley was exactly the same, and as the two of them grew ever more important to the team this led to the skirmishes over who was 'The Man'. It wasn't uncommon for the two of them to be grappling on the floor of the team bus to and from games over who should be the holder of that title in the eyes of the Celtic fans.

Doyley's credentials for the accolade had been well established the season before Frank signed for us. We went to play St Mirren at their old Love Street ground in a Scottish Cup replay that was widely regarded as Johnny's finest ever game in a Celtic jersey.

I'll never forget that night.

Somehow, they got more than twenty-seven thousand people into the ground, with thousands of others locked outside. Mounted police had to shepherd people to safety and the atmosphere was chaotic, which was, I think, how Doyley liked it as a rule.

Tom McAdam was sent off and we were down to ten men for a game that went into extra-time. The Celtic fans were chanting, 'We only need ten men,' because the memory of the league title win over Rangers with that number of players in 1979 was still vivid in the memory. Ironically, it was Doyley who had been sent off that night when I scored the winner in what is forever enshrined in history as the '4–2 game'.

Maybe Johnny was trying to compensate for that experience because he was borderline paranormal in Paisley. He scored twice and ran the home team ragged. He was like a man possessed and the fans were delirious at the end.

Absolutely no one took into account the fact that if it hadn't been for my last-minute equaliser at Celtic Park the previous Saturday there would have been no replay at all. But I have to say there was no other topic of conversation apart from Doyley's display and that was how it should have been. I was just grateful to have played my part in his triumph.

Frank McGarvey came into this environment and immediately started to rattle in the first of his one hundred-plus goals for Celtic. His debut goal was the only one of the match against Rangers at Celtic Park, so the contest to decide who was 'The Man' was therefore declared well and truly open that night.

I didn't like it when opposition players would say to me that Frank was fortunate on the park. They said that he didn't know where he was going when the ball landed at his feet, and because of that, how could defenders know which way to take him on?

All I can say by way of reply to that observation is, I don't think it's possible to score over one hundred goals for your club if you have no idea where you are or what you're about to do next.

Sadly, the internal argument about who was 'The Man' wasn't to be a long-lasting source of fun for all of us in the dressing room. Doyley was taken from us one night in a house in Kilmarnock and all we could do as a club was dedicate the league title win that Frank's goals helped secure for us at the end of that season to Johnny's eternal memory.

The best dressing rooms absorb pain like that and take inspiration from it. Even the sort of almost unendurable pain we were all feeling at that time. They also gather round a teammate who might be undergoing difficulty in his private life and make sure he has collective support.

I'm not breaking any confidences by saying Frank had personal problems to deal with during his playing days. He spoke out about his gambling addiction often, in order to do what he could to prevent others from falling into that trap.

But even those darkest of days can have elements of humour about them.

Davie Provan, Frank and I used to play golf together at the Cardross course near my home. When details of Frank's difficulties first became public, we were there one morning and getting ready to tee-off when Davie ran up to me and said, 'Murdo, remember not to ask Frank what we're playing for.'

We laughed at the memory of that day when Frank visited me in hospital.

It remains the deepest source of personal satisfaction for me that, before he left that day, I swore to Frank I would make it a personal crusade to recover enough strength to repay the compliment and see him while he dealt with his illness.

The essence of team camaraderie is having your mate's back under pressure.

He was there for me. And I was as good as my word to him.

17

Head to Head, Heart to Heart

Ten men won the league and eleven men stopped the Ten.

If you do it by the numbers, that's the only way you could summarise the two most important days of my life at Celtic Park.

I played for the league winners and I was assistant manager of the side that prevented Rangers from creating history with a tenth successive league title.

There are hot topics which would accompany those cold, hard facts, of course. Would the Celtic team of 1979 and the 4–2 game have beaten, or lost to, the Celtic side who won the league in 1998?

My answer to that question is any meeting of the two teams would have ended in a draw, and that is not just diplomacy for the sake of it.

Extraordinary achievements can only come about when there are exceptional people involved in their creation. Would any team containing Danny McGrain, for example, have lost to opposition including Henrik Larsson? It would have to be an honourable share of the points with players of that unique calibre on the park.

And who would, or could, contemplate defeat if they were in a team led by managers of the incredible stature of Billy McNeill or Wim Jansen?

Big Billy replaced the Celtic legend that was Jock Stein, and that was surely the hardest act of all to follow at Celtic. But, to many people, Billy is, was, and forever will be the ultimate Celtic man.

I vividly remember him on the night ten men won the league. He spoke incessantly in the dressing room before our final game of the season got underway.

This was the man who was the first Briton to lift the European Cup. There was nothing complicated about his appointment as manager and no dissent from the Celtic supporters when he came down from Aberdeen to take over from Big Jock.

The fans knew Billy was born for nights like the 4–2 game.

And when Billy moved from one player to the next in the dressing room that night as the minutes ticked down to kick-off, he was shadowed by John Clark, a man who in his own quiet way was always passing on useful bits of advice to young players like me.

I would like to think, with the benefit of hindsight, that I was able to perform a similar function when I was Wim's right-hand man nearly twenty years after that when we were in a similarly delicate situation regarding the outcome of the league championship.

But there was one player who occupied a special place in the squad Wim and I had to work with in our unforgettable championship-campaign season.

Would Celtic have stopped Rangers from rewriting history by winning Ten in a Row if we hadn't brought Henrik Larsson to the club?

I've given that question a lot of thought over the years, and my personal opinion is that the answer would have to be that we would not, and Rangers would have claimed bragging rights that might have lasted a lifetime.

That season was nerve-shredding enough and a strain on mind and body unsurpassed for those who played through it or witnessed the ebb and flow of a title race like no other.

But to have played through it without the one regarded by some supporters as the greatest ever to have worn Celtic's shirt?

I mean absolutely no disrespect to any other player who contributed towards that title win, and there was a heroic level of effort from everyone involved that will be readily acknowledged by every man, woman or child who lived on their nerves for months on end.

But Henrik was the catalyst, the inspiration and the guiding light.

Likewise, I pay unreserved tribute to every player who was my teammate when we won the league in 1979 under circumstances indelible in the mind.

I owe them and the players from 1998 for what they did to give me the memories I treasure from the beginning, and end, of my time at Celtic.

For a bit of harmless fun, and to provoke the kind of debate the fans love, I would offer you this team selected from the people I played beside or worked with as a coach.

The side who won the league in 1979 was:

Peter Latchford;
Danny McGrain and Andy Lynch;

Roy Aitken, Tom McAdam and Johannes Edvaldsson;

Davie Provan, Michael Conroy (Bobby Lennox), George McCluskey, Murdo MacLeod and Johnny Doyle.

The eleven who stopped the Ten were:

Jonathan Gould,

Tom Boyd, Enrico Annoni, Jackie McNamara, Marc Rieper, Alan Stubbs,

Henrik Larsson (Regi Blinker), Craig Burley, Simon Donnelly, Paul Lambert (Morten Wieghorst), Phil O'Donnell (Harald Brattbakk)

From the stellar list of names in those incredible teams, I've chosen my dream team as follows:

JONATHAN GOULD

Gouldie was a big personality who was a magnificent presence for us, on and off the park, when Wim and I were in charge of a season that made exceptional demands on the players at Celtic.

Jonathan had the kind of self-belief that you need around about you in the dressing room if you're going to be successful.

He also played the game with a smile on his face and that came in handy when the psychological toll being demanded of the players on a weekly basis was higher than they had ever known in their careers.

Johnathan earned his place at a time when the club was blessed with other good keepers like Gordon Marshall and Stewart Kerr. And he took his chance after emerging from the reserve team at Bradford City.

142

We lost our first two league games of the season against Hibs and Dunfermline and then Jonathan had an incredible game against St Johnstone in a midweek match in a League Cup tie in Perth. We never looked back after that occasion and Gouldie kept a clean sheet once in every two games.

DANNY McGRAIN

What can you say about this man that is adequate to sum up what he meant to the club?

Danny was a natural leader of men and I walked about Celtic Park in awe of him from the moment I signed from Dumbarton. He could tackle. He could pass the ball and he could win it back for you from the opposition.

Danny had a performance level that never dropped below outstanding from one week to the next. A player who, in his position, was as good as anyone who has ever played for Celtic.

At international level he was such a naturally gifted talent. Danny could move from the right-hand side of the field to the left in order to accommodate the late Sandy Jardine, from Rangers.

That's how good he was in his heyday.

Danny was the main inspiration for me and the others who won the league in 1979.

TOMMY BOYD

Tam gave continuity to the team when Wim and I were assembling our plans for the season that had history in the mix along with the football.

What we wanted to avoid was the disruption to our start in charge. We didn't want to begin with one captain and then find ourselves forced to take a change of direction because we were unsure of the original choice. But there was never any doubt because the man who was captain when we arrived gave us stability of performance and spoke properly to the other players who also needed to have faith in him. There was never any shouting or bad-mouthing, only a steady flow of encouragement for others.

And the bottom line was that Tam was incessantly driven by the fact he had been born with a deep-rooted affection for Celtic, which always comes in handy when you need to go to the well for additional levels of determination.

ROY AITKEN

Here we are talking about a force of nature.

Big Roy had strength, speed and the ability to bring those qualities into play no matter what area of the park he happened to be in at the time. What made him extra special was that he could score goals into the bargain. Roy would also take personal responsibility for charging forward from the back if he thought there was an opportunity to take advantage of space he could see was open to exploitation.

I think back to the Scottish Cup final in 1985 when we were tied at 1–1 against Dundee United and the final whistle wasn't that far away. Roy was always extremely vocal and he was telling all of us on the park that there was still time to win the game. The big guy was as good as his word. It was Roy who threw over the cross from the right wing that Frank McGarvey dived to meet and head the goal that took the trophy.

On that day, like so many others when I marvelled at him, Roy lifted the team by sheer strength of will.

MARC RIEPER

In the season when Celtic had to stop Rangers from doing something that might never be repeated, it felt as if we were all being held captive in a challenging place. It was a supreme, and prolonged, test of your psychological capabilities.

Marc showed from the outset that he was capable of living with that kind of pressure on a daily basis. He wasn't Scottish but he fully understood what he was involved in and he responded by going about his work in a way that wasn't fussy but was always consistent in terms of his application. He was a big unit and a strong, uncompromising tackler at the back, as well as being a popular personality within the group.

Marc 'got' the club and you need people like that if you're facing what was seen as the ultimate challenge for the players.

It looked as if there was an element of fate about Marc's time with us. In October 1998 he suffered a toe injury which meant he would never again play for Celtic, but he had, over the course of just thirty-seven appearances, made a lasting imprint on the club's history.

PAUL LAMBERT

I was directly involved in the move that took Paul to Borussia Dortmund when his contract expired at

Motherwell. A move that led to him becoming a European Cup winner before returning to Scotland and entering Celtic folklore.

I got a telephone call one day from Michael Henke, who was then assistant to Dortmund's head coach, Ottmar Hitzfeld. He wanted to know what I thought of Paul's ability to make the move from Scotland, as I had once done, to the Bundesliga. My input was based on the time I had spent working with Paul at international gatherings during my time as a member of the SFA's coaching staff.

My recommendation, which was glowing, was built around the fact that Paul was brilliant at taking the ball and passing it on in a way I knew would be perfect for German football. I was asking my old club to trust my judgement on his attributes and sign him without reservation.

Germany was the making of Paul. He went to the right place at the right time and achieved something very special.

Paul had been to the mountaintop and then came back home and immersed himself in a situation that was anything but easy, particularly since he arrived after the season had started.

In the end, though, he made a material difference to the outcome of that championship, as evidenced by one winning goal against Rangers at Celtic Park that altered the course of the season.

CRAIG BURLEY

Craig scored the other goal that day against Rangers when the New Year got off to an optimistic start. Burley was different class for us. He had previously been at

Chelsea and was therefore used to playing the game at a very high level.

As important was the fact that he was a chirpy figure who brought an upbeat influence to the team.

The game comes naturally to gifted players and Craig was a terrific signing for Wim and me. He was a fighter for the team and scored a lot of great goals in the season like no other.

MURDO MACLEOD

It's my book and I'm picking the team!

I still laugh when I think about the newspaper quote from Billy McNeill which made headlines immediately before Davie Provan and I made our sudden arrival at Celtic Park.

Hearts had beaten Celtic at Tynecastle at a time when a championship win looked unlikely for the big man in his first season back at the club. Billy was asked the standard question about what injuries he might have ahead of the next game, which happened to be against Motherwell. It is as unthreatening a question as you're ever likely to get, but Billy was obviously in no mood for small talk.

'How would they get injured?' he said. 'Getting out of the (expletive deleted) bath?'

It was the kind of remark made by a man at the end of his tether and in need of a change of direction.

That verbal exchange took place on the Saturday evening in Edinburgh. Davie and I were signed, sealed and delivered to Celtic Park by the following Wednesday. I like to think we changed the dynamic of the season by bringing a youthful, and fresh, perspective.

In 2019 I organised a dinner for the survivors of the 4–2 game and it was a special night for all of us gathered in a restaurant in Glasgow. Sadly, big Billy was no longer with us by then, having passed away in April of that year.

Johnny Doyle was gone and so too was Johannes Edvaldsson.

We toasted their memory and then we worked out how we, and they, had managed to win the league from an unpromising position.

If you're talking about the final, and decisive, match then it's quite simple, really. If you are numerically disadvantaged then you run harder and you work harder. And, because you are playing Rangers and the league title is at stake, then you try harder than you have ever done in your life.

And then, if you're fortunate, you score the winning goal!

DAVIE PROVAN

Players who wear their socks down at their ankles aren't making a fashion statement. They are extending an open invitation to opposition defenders to paint their legs black and blue.

Davie was a regular target for the kind of physical abuse that could be excessive in the season we won the league. But he was always brave enough to withstand the heavy stuff and keep coming back for more while somehow maintaining a level of artistry on the wing that was a pleasure to watch and a constant source of supply for teammates who thrived off his final ball.

Davie was arguably one of the last great crossers of a ball in Scottish football. He certainly made a lot of goals for me because of that particular talent, which now has the look of a dying art about it.

I always felt a special bond with Davie because we arrived in the same week from smaller clubs, Dumbarton and Kilmarnock, and quickly showed we could handle the step up a level.

HENRIK LARSSON

There can be no praise higher than to say I don't think Celtic would have won the league, and stopped Rangers from winning Ten in a Row, if Henrik had not been in the team. The decision to go for the player who arrived from the Netherlands as a mere mortal and left Scotland as the undisputed King of Kings in the eyes of the Celtic fans will go down in history as the single most important bit of business Wim Jansen ever carried out on Celtic's behalf.

The fact that we remain friends to this day speaks volumes for the camaraderie that sustained Celtic throughout the season, and Henrik made an indelible impression on the minds of a generation of supporters.

Each fan will retain a special memory, a particular goal or match that helped set Henrik apart. I would quibble with none of the choices made by anyone.

He was quite simply a player without peer.

GEORGE McCLUSKEY

The modern way to assess a player's contribution to any side is to look at his numbers. George was born to play with, and score goals for Celtic.

His numbers were also sprinkled with stardust.

The fact that he did it so often on the big occasions when it really mattered was what made him an invaluable teammate.

George scored in the 4–2 game.

He had the touch that diverted the ball away from Rangers' goalkeeper, Peter McCloy, to win the Scottish Cup final a year later.

And he scored one of the goals which won the league on the final day of the season in 1982, one of three league title wins George would be part of as a Celtic player.

He was as deadly as he was dedicated to being the best he could be in a Celtic jersey.

In other words, the kind of teammate you want standing beside you in the tunnel when you're about to go on to the pitch.

★

It takes a special mentality to wear Celtic's strip. That's why the legendary Jock Stein said the jersey wouldn't shrink to accommodate lesser individuals.

Those I have left out were not unsuitable for selection. I stand by the managerial cliché that I can only pick eleven at a time.

And I salute every one of those who stood by me in every tunnel before we went out to give our all for the club.

18

Bogey Men

THERE ARE TWO GROUPS of people whose contribution to the game in this country is summed up in just two words by the majority of supporters. The groups I'm referring to are referees and the media. The bogey men of Scottish football.

And the couple of words I'm talking about are not the offensive ones you might have thought of first of all. But they do adequately convey the degree of negativity directed towards match officials and those who cover the game for newspapers, radio and television.

Beneath contempt.

I have dealt with referees as a player, coach and manager over three decades and I spent twelve years of my life working in the media after stepping back from football's front line, so I think I'm well qualified to assess the work of all concerned.

The two groups are connected by an approach to their work that causes them to be held in contempt. Fans believe that there are certain teams which are given a hard time by match officials and the press and others that are protected by them. The supporters who feel that way don't think there is such a thing as a level playing field.

And they want safeguards put in place to protect their team's best interests, such as a register of match officials in which their boyhood allegiances are declared and their suitability for handling certain matches is assessed from that perspective.

Let me state straight away that I consider that idea to be unworthy of consideration, based on my time with Celtic as player and coach. I shared a dressing room during some of the club's greatest years with teammates who had not come from homes where Celtic was the club they had been brought up to support. All of that changed when they signed for Celtic and started to dedicate their lives to making the team, and the club, the best it could be.

I'm thinking about the likes of legendary figures such as Kenny Dalglish and Danny McGrain. And the greatest of all of them, Jock Stein, the man who created the modern-day Celtic in the 1960s by winning the European Cup and creating a record within the domestic game by winning the first Nine in a Row.

It would be an insult to their memory to say that a family background with a different club would have made them suspicious in anyone's eyes. And an affront to a club that is inclusive and has always tried to be that way.

Let me say there were referees, and linesmen, I was wary of when I played for Celtic. There were decisions against me in particular, or the team in general, that I found difficult to understand. But I would rather have played in the era I did than be part of the game today.

We live in a climate of suspicion, and I think VAR has helped create that mood which surrounds the game. The

Video Assistant Referee has taken the joy out of football and the actual match referee is not in control of anything any more, which is to the detriment of the game as a whole so far as I can see.

They are letting VAR do their job for them because their decision is no longer final, as it was in my day, and fans are disillusioned when a monitor dictates that a toe over a line when it's drawn on a screen means that a goal should be deemed illegal and chalked off. It may, in the very strictest sense, be offside, but is it really in the spirit of the game?

I'm not in favour of drawing up a list which makes certain referees unsuitable for matches because of who they supported when they were still at school. I can't convince myself that's the right thing to do.

Who would handle an Old Firm game if that register of referees existed? Everyone would be excluded for one reason or another.

Likewise, the notion of former players becoming referees is understandable in principle, but what chance would a former Celtic or Rangers player have of being accepted in our climate of suspicion? How could they be given control of a match involving their former club without having their integrity immediately called into question?

I would simply like to see today's referees take greater responsibility for their own actions on the park and get a stronger grip on making up their own minds about the big calls they have to make.

You will never convince some fans that referees take a fully professional, unbiased approach to their work and don't play favourites, but all I can say is I never stood in a tunnel preparing to take the field for a match while thinking the referee was going to do everything in his power to cheat me out of a result.

In nine years at Celtic as a player, I was never once sent off and I played a robust style of game which involved being strong in the challenge for the ball and open to scrutiny by referees.

And the press.

I always think of Billy McNeill when the subject of press coverage and referees' performance levels comes up. Big Billy didn't need any registers to inform him about anything. He could tell you the name of every journalist he suspected of not having Celtic's best interests at heart and what they had said about us when I was playing under him in my formative years at Celtic Park. And he could get quite worked up about it while making his feelings abundantly clear to those who had annoyed him; referees or members of the media.

From what I saw of Ange Postecoglou at Celtic Park, he always came across as being very calm and self-assured in front of the press in any of its shapes or forms. He seemed happier to analyse football matches rather than get embroiled in controversy.

Managers come and go, but the reaction to their work, or that of their successors, is always the same.

The media are quick to judge.

In the space of our first two weeks at the start of the season in which Celtic won the league and stopped Rangers from winning Ten in a Row in 1998, they would have had you believe Henrik Larsson was a poor signing and Wim Jansen was a seriously bad appointment as manager.

You can't get much more premature than that.

Henrik had made a single bad pass that led to Hibs scoring the winning goal against us at Easter Road on the opening day of the league championship and Wim's unsuitability for his role was based on losing that match and the one that followed at home to Dunfermline.

I can tell you for a fact that neither Henrik nor Wim ever spoke to me about a press campaign being waged against them that season.

It was many years after he'd gone from Celtic Park that Henrik joked with me about the hysteria which had come after the opening-day defeat in Edinburgh.

The truth of the matter is we focused so hard on winning the title that there was no time to pay any attention to the press coverage of what was going on.

Wim was bigger than falling out with any journalist over what had been written, or said, about him. That's why he would never ask me to do his press duties for him. He was confident in what he was doing and never spoke in headlines in any case.

We knew, in spite of what anybody in the media said about us, that Celtic would win the title. It was a confidence based entirely on the fact we believed implicitly that we had a team who were better than Rangers.

But when I went into the media on a regular basis, I always valued my own integrity over the fact I had played for, and helped manage, Celtic. I would never have refused to praise any Rangers player because I had once been employed by their greatest rivals. I would have thought less of myself if I had acted in any other way.

At the end of the day, supporters know what they're looking at out on the park. If I, or anybody else, had tried to pull the wool over their eyes because of personal bias then they would have instinctively known they were being fed questionable comments and my credibility would have been diminished as a consequence.

I don't mean this to be insulting to any media person who has not played football professionally, but I honestly think former players are better at analysing games and understanding the guys on the park. That's why there are so many of them involved in journalistic work today.

They are more tolerant and patient than others because they know what that player on the park is going through and how they'll be feeling at any given moment. That's not to say the people in the press box can't have an opinion that is valid, but it helps sometimes to have been at the sharp end of the game at the highest level.

At the same time, there is no denying there are some former players who would have to acknowledge the accusation that they can, on occasion, be more like cheerleaders than commentators on the game. They let previous allegiances get in the way of sound judgement. They'll know who they are.

They want supporters to think well of them rather than avoiding that trap and saying what they think without fear or favour. And some feel the need to draw attention to themselves by what they say, which was never my understanding of how I should go about my business.

If I had ever been accused of bias when I was working for BBC Scotland I would have answered that allegation by counter-accusing my critic of selective hearing, because I don't believe I was ever guilty of that particular offence.

I would never have been happy to be thought of, and dismissed, as a wind-up merchant.

Radio phone-in programmes can be a useful barometer of public opinion on everything to do with the game, but sometimes you have to exercise personal judgement and put to one side what certain callers say.

When he was Celtic manager, Gordon Strachan used to say it was the quality of the criticism that counted. I think he meant that you had to tell the difference between what was objective criticism and what was anger-driven rhetoric.

I know a load of baloney when I hear it coming from former players, and so will the listeners or viewers. The majority, it should be said in fairness, are good at what they do.

They know, for example, that, after watching a World Cup in full, you can't measure all of the players in this country against the ones you've just watched in the biggest tournament of all. That would be unrealistic. Former players have been in the shoes of the present-day players, and they get what these performers are trying to achieve and the heights they are capable of reaching.

In the final analysis, it's desirable, and beneficial, to have a good relationship with referees and the media. But this is Scotland and that's not always going to be the case.

The only thing you can hope for is that everyone carries out their professional duties to the best of their ability and treats others with equal fairness.

People can always look back on what was said about Henrik and Wim and appreciate that hysterical reaction will always be found out in the end.

19

Ange and the
Lessons Learned

I MET ANGE POSTECOGLOU for the first time when I went to Celtic Park before Frank McGarvey's funeral in January 2020. The club had provided buses that were to take Frank's 1980s teammates, and their families, to his Requiem Mass in a church on the outskirts of Glasgow.

I was boarding the bus when I saw an outstretched hand waiting to shake mine and heard a distinctive voice call me by my first name. It was Ange.

How he recognised me I don't know, but he was immediately engaging and keen to know how I was progressing after my release from hospital. It was overwhelming for me, my wife and two of our daughters who were with me. After the church service was over, Ange spoke to us again before we went back to Celtic Park for a gathering of old faces.

I told him that, when he was appointed as manager at Celtic Park, I was telephoned by a radio station in Sydney and asked what I thought of the club's decision to hire someone who was unknown to the supporters.

I told them, as I told Ange, that I had in-depth experience of these matters. My verdict was that if Ange beat

Rangers to the league title he would become an iconic figure, recognised and thanked wherever he went in the world after his time in Scotland was over. I knew that would be the case because I had watched the same thing happen to Wim Jansen a quarter of a century earlier. The similarities between the two stories are remarkable.

Wim went to Celtic from a club in Japan, and so did Ange.

Wim had a terrific eye for a player and his dealings in the transfer market were as quick as they were profitable. Just like Ange.

I'm not making direct comparisons between the two players, but if I say Henrik Larsson and Kyogo Furuhashi quickly became inspirational figures, that's the quick way to understand what insider knowledge can do for you.

Wim knew the marketplace, and who was available, in his native Holland. Ange had an encyclopaedic knowledge of the Asian market because he'd worked in the J-League.

Wim and Ange also came to Scotland on their own but had the strength of will to make that an irrelevant detail while getting about the job they were hired to do, and being spectacularly successful in a short space of time.

Both men won a league title at Rangers' expense and that was tribute to their man-management skills.

I obviously observed Wim at close quarters as his right-hand man, but on that first day I met Ange I readily understood he had the same kind of qualities Wim possessed. He was the kind of guy you would run through the proverbial brick wall to impress if you were a player. I'd played for Billy McNeill and I had coached with Wim. I knew about these things on an instinctive basis.

Wim and Ange even shared an unsteady start to the seasons in which they won the championship. We lost our first two league games, home and away, at the start of the season Wim and I had together in 1997/98. Ange lost three of his first six games in 2021, also to the sound of alarm bells going off in the background.

Both men had the self-belief and the inner strength to turn a deaf ear to the noise and get on with what they knew was the right thing to do. They made club management look easy which I knew from personal experience was anything but the case.

I learned my lesson the hard way.

I got together with Wim relatively soon after coming off the toughest season I had known in football. The season I managed Partick Thistle.

In 1995 I had won promotion as player-manager at Dumbarton, the club where I had started my professional career. Then the manager's job at Firhill became vacant when John Lambie decided to take up an offer he had received from Falkirk to go there.

John was, and still is to this day, a legendary figure in Partick Thistle's history. Indivisible from the club's name even though he is no longer with us.

But when I was approached by the then Firhill chairman, Jim Oliver, I wasn't worried in the slightest about following the toughest act of all in Maryhill. I just wanted to manage a full-time club at the highest level of the game in Scotland.

Dumbarton were initially reluctant to let me go but we eventually parted on good terms and there can't have been any residual ill-feeling because I have since been inducted into the club's Hall of Fame and I've got the framed certificate to prove it.

Partick Thistle will forever be the other club in Glasgow, permanently in the shadow of Celtic and

Rangers, because they can't begin to live with either club in terms of the financial resources that enable them to bring in players of a higher quality than can ever find their way to Firhill.

In the season I was there, for example, I took the team to play Celtic and the kick-off to the game was delayed by what I thought was an extraordinary length of time.

While I was growing more and more agitated in the dugout, I noticed a commotion at the mouth of the tunnel and out came the Portuguese legend, Jorge Cadete, to be introduced to the crowd as Celtic's latest signing.

In the midst of the bedlam I'm thinking to myself, 'What chance have you got?'

Celtic brought in Cadete and still didn't win the league title, which they would not do until Wim and I got there two years later.

Before that happened, though, I had to endure all sorts at Firhill. When you go to a full-time club from part-time surroundings it's great to have a full squad to work with on a daily basis, but you also have to shoulder everyone's problems and grievances when you're the manager. Everything from childcare issues to players angrily knocking on your door while looking for a reason why they've not been picked for this game or that one.

The trouble-makers you can spot from a mile away. The remedy is to leave them out of the team so that they know the manager has perfect eyesight and is displeased.

When you're at a club like Celtic you are working with a better class of player. That's not intended as an insult to honest professionals at other clubs. It simply stands to reason that Celtic can afford to shop at a higher level of the player market. What I needed to compensate for a financial gap that I, or the club, couldn't bridge was grafters in my team.

During that season at Firhill I should have played in the team myself on a more regular basis. I know that now with the benefit of hindsight. I could have talked the players through what I wanted from them from a closer proximity than the touchline. In actual fact, I only played one game, against Aberdeen at Pittodrie on 21 October 1995, and that ended in a 3–0 defeat.

I have put the date down for posterity because that was the end of Murdo MacLeod the football player. It was my last ever competitive match and brought to an end a career that had started with a reserve game for Dumbarton down the road in Dundee at Dens Park twenty years earlier.

I didn't have any time for sentimentality that day when the final whistle blew at Pittodrie because this was a season that would end with a play-off final between Dundee United and Partick Thistle to see who played in the Premier League and who would be in the division below.

It would end in a game that gave me one of the lowest moments I had ever known in football and drove a wedge between me and the match referee, a man called Les Mottram. A rift that will never heal.

I know football can be a cruel game at times, but I had played literally hundreds of matches in my career and I had never known anything like the carry-on that took place at Tannadice on the night of 16 May 1996.

I didn't take a conscious decision to be on my best behaviour whatever the game threw at me over the years. It was the way I approached my life in football. If something bad happens to your team then you can't ask for the match to be played again. There's nothing that can be done if a result doesn't suit you.

When it's gone, it's gone.

But that season at Partick Thistle tried my patience to the extreme.

There was a bust-up in the tunnel at Brockville when we played John Lambie's Falkirk, ironically enough, but an SFA hearing concluded that I didn't deserve to be punished for any of what went on after one player from each side had been sent off.

And then came Tannadice and the play-off decider.

We had drawn with United at Firhill in the first leg of the final the previous Sunday in front of a crowd of more than ten thousand people. There was a crowd of over twelve thousand fans in Dundee and the match was as dramatic as it deserved to be.

Thistle took the lead from the penalty spot and Ian Cameron's goal was no more than we deserved. We were dominating a home team that had some terrific names in it. They had the likes of Steven Pressley, Christian Dailly, Maurice Malpas, Andy McLaren, Robbie Winters and Owen Coyle, but we were all over them. We had a clear-cut penalty denied us to create a two-goal lead that would have been enough to win the match and keep us in the top flight.

Mottram had, a couple of years earlier, been involved in a bizarre incident at Firhill when Dundee United scored a perfectly good goal and he missed the moment and let play go on. The ball had been struck so ferociously it had rebounded from the stanchion at the back of the net and fallen into the arms of the goalkeeper. The Thistle players were literally throwing the ball to each other when they realised the referee, Mottram, was waving play on. Clearly the linesman had missed it too as there was no flag.

The United bench went mad and one or two of them were actually on the park, but no goal was given and play continued.

Incredible.

I couldn't begin to prove that famous day had any influence over Mottram when he denied us the penalty claim at Tannadice, but the non-award changed the course of the game.

One of the reasons why I should have played more for Thistle was that I could have talked my players through game management. We were deep into injury time and had the ball out at the corner flag in our half of the field. It should have been easy to run down the clock from there but, instead, we lost possession and Brian Welsh scored an equaliser to send the tie into extra-time.

United had brought on Coyle, a prolific goalscorer everywhere he went, shortly before then and he had to be the one who popped up with five minutes left to play and scored the goal that relegated the Jags.

The irony was I had known Owen since he was a teenager and liked him very much. He and his two brothers were at Dumbarton during my formative years there and I always had time for him.

There was no point in getting angry with Owen because he'd scored the decisive goal. My anger was reserved for a referee who had given my team one penalty but had decided he couldn't possibly give us two.

Years later I saw Mottram at a game and he tried to wave over to me in a cheery fashion, but I don't mind admitting I blanked him. And I would do the same thing if I saw him again at any time in the future. I am definitely not vindictive by nature, but I do believe match officials have a professional responsibility to get the big decisions correct, and my opinion remains that he failed in that obligation at Tannadice. It cost Thistle their league status and it ultimately cost me my job.

My wife tells a story that when I came home to break the news to my family, our youngest daughter, Marina, who was nearly four years old at the time, went out to the front garden and shouted to the lady who owned a house across the road from us, 'My daddy got the sack,' at the top of her voice.

That's life in football for you, and I will always look back on my time in the game with nothing but a sense of satisfaction. I played for great clubs and won lots of trophies with them in two different countries. I have absolutely no regrets about anything other than that night at Tannadice as a manager, but in football, as in life, you must always move on.

I will be eternally grateful to Big Billy for allowing me to play for a club like Celtic and everything he did for me when he and I were there together.

I owe Hörst Koppel and Reinhard Saftig, my coaches in Germany, for all they did for me at Borussia Dortmund.

And there are no words of thanks sincere enough to explain my gratitude to Wim Jansen for making me his assistant at Celtic and allowing me to be part of a season that is now enshrined in the club's folklore.

If I had stayed longer than my nine years as a player at Celtic Park I might have fulfilled my dream to become the manager there one day. Who knows?

If I had accepted the contractual offer to extend my time at Borussia Dortmund by another four years I might never have come back from Germany and might have made my life there as a coach when the playing days were over. We had a home that was big enough to make an extended stay no problem at all, but we came home to let the girls further their education in Scotland.

Life has presented me with medical trials and tribulations since I retired from football, and I am still dealing with the consequences of illness, but there is always a need to retain a sense of perspective.

I have twice in later life been in what you might call the touch-and-go department and I have been fortunate enough to come out on the right side on both occasions. Others who were great friends have not been so lucky and I will always remember them fondly.

I also know I have been spared because others would not let me go. They know who they are and how much I think of them.

20

Hospital

KNOWING THAT THERE ARE PEOPLE in this world who would do anything for you is a very special feeling. There's nothing I'd change about my career in football, which has brought me more in life than I could ever have hoped for as a young lad growing up in the suburbs of Glasgow. The issues with my health have been well documented and, as I've said, they have been very challenging both for me and my close family, who mean everything to me.

Getting out of hospital in 2023 was a big moment for me and for all of us. I knew my ordeal by ventilator was over and my re-entry into the world I had almost left behind was underway when my daughter, Mhairi, came to the hospital to collect me in her soft-top Mini and take me away from my 103-day stay on NHS orders.

Autumn was moving towards winter and the car was transporting me from Glasgow to our home in Rhu. As we drove along the seafront in Helensburgh, close to our final destination, Mhairi let the roof down and I felt the cold air hit my face in a moment that symbolised a return to normality for me.

It was an exhilarating experience in more ways than one.

I couldn't be complimentary enough when it comes to the hospital staff who looked after me. Doctors, nurses, anyone who had anything to do with my time in two hospitals, I can't thank you enough for what you did and will be forever in awe of your care, attention and compassion.

But the moment the fresh air stung my face was enough to make me feel like a hostage who had been released from captivity and was looking forward to rehabilitation in the company of his family.

Medical help had given me the ability to grow old instead of my life being cut short, but what happened in the days, weeks and months that followed my return from hospital allowed me to understand that former football players who have had the good fortune to have been with a club like Celtic don't actually grow old. They are frozen in time in the minds of the supporters who remember them in their prime and have cherished memories of a certain game, or goal, that live with them.

When I made public the details of what I had been through while clinging to life, the response was astounding on a global basis. To this day I have a Celtic fan in Australia, a man I have never met called Gerry Connelly, who sends me, on a regular basis, photographs of me during a match or in a team group. The early 1980s appear to be his favourite time watching the team and I am an integral part of his recollections.

I did think hard about whether or not I should go public about my health issues, and about how much detail I should divulge. When you're facing a life-or-death situation all sorts of things can happen that you've never,

ever thought about before. I felt I owed it to people who I'd never met but were still offering me such fantastic support, and were keeping my spirits up, to let them know how I was doing and to continue to be honest with them, as I have always been.

One of the strangest things I had to deal with was when my toes started to drop off. The first toe to drop off, or self-amputate as they say to make it sound less graphic, came away from me on 22 February 2023.

Others would follow over the course of time until there were none left.

I wasn't traumatised by the event, and I didn't even feel a thing. I was asked by the podiatrist who was dealing with me at a clinic in Helensburgh that morning, if I wanted to take the toe away with me. I think the lady believed she was asking me a rhetorical question for a bit of fun, so she was shocked when I asked her to put it an envelope.

I wasn't being ghoulish. I knew then and now what's ahead of me in terms of regaining a better state of health after being on a ventilator in hospital for eight weeks and I wanted to keep the toe to symbolise the next phase of my recovery. It's a permanent reminder of where I've been and where I'm headed now, so far as my recovery is concerned.

It was an odd day, really. The sun was shining and the view over the water in Helensburgh was stunning. My wife and I stopped on the way home to buy carrot cake, if I remember correctly, and then we told our daughters what had happened.

The time spent on the machine that was saving my life after heart surgery has left me suffering from something called necrosis. The blood that was directed towards my vital organs as I lay unconscious on the ventilator was not getting to my toes and when that happens body tissues die. I didn't feel a thing because there is nothing to feel at the end of my feet.

The process is irreversible.

I will now wait until the rest of the toes self-amputate and then investigate where I go from there and what can be done to help me compensate for what has happened.

In the meantime, I have to endure. It is for me, without being melodramatic, a life of pain. And that means taking a lot of painkillers to cope with the discomfort all over my feet. I can't have a normal life back again until something can be done about that area of my body.

I'll be seen by doctors and nurses every week for the foreseeable future and, in the meantime, I have to come to terms with the kind of inactivity I haven't been used to before in my life.

None of this has left me dealing with depression because I need to stay psychologically strong to deal with what lies ahead of me. You can't become overwhelmed, even when they tell you that I could take my socks off one night and find a toe, or toes, inside them. It's not a happy time. How could it be under the circumstances? I'm involved in a battle and I will have to fight this problem with every fibre of my being.

But, as I've said, in football and in life you have to keep moving on as best you can in the circumstances you're facing. That might mean moving on from a club when you really wanted to stay, or finding new ways to move on with your life as you adapt to a new situation.

And so, a few months after my release from hospital, it was time for my first night out in the company of friends and when it came time for me to leave the restaurant in Glasgow city centre, the taxi driver taking me home instantly recognised his passenger.

'Murdo MacLeod,' he said. 'I didn't know it was you I was coming to pick up.'

What he also didn't know was that the step that was supposed to help me up into his taxi wasn't working properly and, being on crutches at the time, I couldn't get into his vehicle to sit down properly.

Once we came to an understanding of the situation and I was able to get into the taxi, we talked non-stop about games I had played in for Celtic throughout the course of a forty-five-minute journey home. What had happened to me, the difference in my physical make-up – it was as if none of that had ever taken place so far as the driver was concerned. I was the one who had played for Celtic, scored important goals against Rangers and was enshrined in the driver's memory for that reason.

It was a gratifying exchange and it is people like that who have got me through my medical problems and kept me going during my yet-to-be-completed recovery.

I like to think I always gave people my time on a voluntary basis throughout my career and now they return the compliment to me at a period in my life when I take great comfort from their interest.

There was a daily ritual at Borussia Dortmund which saw the first team players sign forty or so footballs that had been carefully laid out in the dressing room for us to autograph for the team's fans.

For the most part, it meant a series of squiggles hastily scrawled on the ball, but I always made a point of painstakingly signing my name properly as a mark of respect for the people who gave the players their backing on match days.

I knew there were people coming into my hospital room as I lay there, day after day, who were only putting their heads around the door because they'd been told who was occupying that particular bed, but it didn't bother me. They were just being nice.

My problem was that, over the course of that very long journey from diagnosis to surgery, and what came after, I wasn't always compos mentis. I couldn't even be given a sip of water in case that caused me to choke, so my mouth was dabbed by swabs as my weight plummeted due to my inability to eat.

I personally don't remember this particular incident happening, but my wife, Mhairi, assures me there was one day, when I was in a delirious state of mind, that I asked a family relative if he could open the window in the room so that I could make my escape from the hospital. I told her of my annoyance that he refused to do what I had asked him to do and she pointed out that he had declined to comply with my wishes for one very good reason.

If my room had been on the ground floor of the building then my breakout plan might have had a semblance of a chance of coming off. But I was on the third floor of the hospital and leaving by the window would assuredly have had fatal consequences. I was drifting in and out of consciousness and there were days when I obviously had to be saved from myself.

Once I left the hospital by the front door and not via a third-floor window, I was involved in a challenge to get back on my own two feet. I knew the process was succeeding when I was invited by Michael Nicholson, Celtic's chief executive, to watch my first game at Celtic Park since becoming seriously unwell. It also happened to be Brendan

Rodgers' first game at home after rejoining the club as Ange Postecoglou's successor in the manager's office.

Brendan's reappointment had been the cause of huge controversy with some supporters being unhappy over his re-engagement because he had left Celtic, years earlier, when the season had still to finish in order to join Leicester City.

I had a simple analysis of Brendan's return to Glasgow.

If the Rangers supporters had hoped he wouldn't take the job for a second time, on the grounds that he is a first-class coach who was a threat to their team's prospects of success, then the Celtic fans should have welcomed his decision to come back with open arms.

But some, like the fan I met while out with my wife near our home one day, were harder than others to convince that my argument was sound. The supporter told me he had a season ticket at Celtic Park and would continue to renew the ticket for the duration of Brendan's three-year, contractually agreed stay. But he assured me he would not enter the ground during the lifetime of that contract.

Fans can sometimes get ideas inside their heads that aren't quite accurate, to my way of thinking.

Another one is that club directors aren't real supporters of the club like them and don't feel the highs and the lows the way they do. I can say, from the personal experience of having been a guest of the club in the boardroom at Celtic Park since coming out of hospital, that that is simply not the case.

I have observed the chairman, Peter Lawwell, Michael Nicholson and directors like Michael McDonald before and after matches and, believe me, they feel it like the men, women and children spread throughout the ground in Celtic scarves.

I revelled in that first day back as I saw faces I had known around Celtic Park for years and fed off their best wishes. Celtic were playing Ross County and the day became even more emotional for me when I met the County manager, Malky Mackay, after the game.

Malky had been part of the squad who won the league for Celtic and stopped Rangers from getting Ten in a Row when Wim Jansen and I were the management team.

I was back to being frozen in time because that day and that landmark game against St Johnstone was all people wanted to talk about when they introduced themselves to me. Apart from anything else, I was grateful those conversations stimulated the mind as I gradually got over that lengthy period when I was attached to machines in hospital while being unconscious.

I've been back since then at the club's invitation and brought myself up to date while watching my grandson, Fergus, have his photograph taken with Kyogo Furuhashi.

One day, far into the future, someone will stop Kyogo in a Japanese street and talk to him about Celtic.

We are all frozen in time and should be glad about it.

I know I am.

21
Mhairi's Story

ON TWO SEPARATE OCCASIONS in my life, spread over a twelve-year period, I have been taken into the same family room, inside the same hospital, and solemnly been told there's a chance my husband won't leave the building alive because he hasn't been able to survive the aftermath of heart surgery.

But my husband's name is Murdo MacLeod and during the nine years he spent playing for Celtic he was known to the supporters and his teammates as the Rhino.

There were reasons behind that nickname.

It was a tribute to Murdo's physical strength, mental fortitude and bloody-minded determination, which gave him an iron will to enable him to overcome any form of adversity.

We were married when we were no more than kids ourselves and raised a family to be proud of. He was good enough as a part-time player at Dumbarton to be signed for Celtic for what was then a large sum of money and he won every domestic honour there was at the club before pursuing his career elsewhere.

We moved to a foreign country and assimilated ourselves into the German way of life while Murdo was at Borussia

Dortmund. And then we came home again to see my husband enter the next phase of his life, winning trophies as a player at Hibs, a manager at Dumbarton and, most memorable of all, as Wim Jansen's coach when Celtic won the league title that prevented Rangers from getting Ten in a Row.

You don't stand back and allow that kind of man to slip away from this life, and especially not when he and I raised a family of girls who formed a protective shield around their father and refused to accept that medical opinion was necessarily the final word on his mortality.

In October 2022, I assembled that family around about me in the room at the Jubilee Hospital in Clydebank, which specialises in heart problems, so that the medical staff there could update us on Murdo's condition.

There present was a female doctor and a male anaes-thetist. I remember thinking one was doom and the other one was gloom.

Neither of them truly knew the Rhino.

First of all we were asked if we wanted to have a husband and a father suffering from heart and kidney failure to be put back on a ventilator and attached to a dialysis machine. The doctors and nurses couldn't waken Murdo from his state of unconsciousness and the thin line between life and death was outlined to us in matter-of-fact detail.

Murdo's brain needed to start functioning properly for him to come back to us and all forms of medication designed to address that situation had failed miserably. It was suggested to us that my husband and the girls' father was not intended to waken up and that medical statistics dictated his chances of pulling through were slim.

In other words, the clock was ticking on his time on earth.

Murdo's heart wasn't functioning. His kidneys weren't functioning. We were witnessing a tightrope walk between life and death. Then the silence was broken and our daughter, Mhairi, altered the mood inside that family room with a message to the medical staff that was part defiance and part positivity.

'We hear you,' she said, 'but we're just not listening to you. We're ignoring you because that's Murdo MacLeod in there.'

High dependency was one thing. Low tolerance of the idea that throwing in the towel was an option was another thing altogether.

We created life. We nurtured life. And we weren't the kind of people to give up on life. Our daughters wouldn't have allowed me to even contemplate the idea, even if Murdo's heart difficulties over a lengthy period of time had, ironically, led to me developing problems of my own in that direction.

It was all so different when I worked part-time as a teenager at a petrol station not far from Dumbarton's former home at Boghead. The garage had a shop where I worked behind the till and the young Dumbarton hopefuls would go in there for the confectionary that kept them going.

I kept him at arm's length at first because I was the older woman, being all of nine months his senior. But that old persistence of his came into play and he kept coming in to give me the benefit of his chat-up lines.

I gave in eventually and we got married on 11 June 1977.

It didn't take me long to find out what life as a footballer's wife would be like because it was enacted in full view of the public.

Murdo went to sign for Celtic on the same day in 1978 that a man had been at our house in Dumbarton to measure the windows for venetian blinds. He was the grumpiest man in the world as he went about his business. By the time he came back to fit the blinds, Murdo's photograph had been on the back pages of all the newspapers holding a Celtic scarf above his head to mark his signing for Billy McNeill. And the grumpiest man in the world had magically been transformed into the friendliest man in the world. We assumed he was a Celtic fan and that was how life would be from then on.

I had only been to one football match before we got married and that was when one of my primary school teachers had taken the pupils who were interested to watch the Sons, as Dumbarton were known, play at Boghead.

But Celtic Park was a different story.

Celtic beat Rangers to win the league title at the end of Murdo's first season there, and the memory of the night they beat Rangers in the final game of the season to become champions lives with me to this day.

I became engrossed and I grew more like my husband by believing anything was possible for Celtic.

Strangely enough, when Murdo was managing Dumbarton in later years and trying to win the club promotion, I used to get so stressed out I had to have massage therapy to relax my body, but I just had this feeling that Celtic were capable of anything. That's why I was the only player's wife to go to the match against St Mirren in Paisley that won another title against all the odds in 1986.

It was the last day of the season and Hearts only had to draw against Dundee away to pip Davie Hay's side at the post for the championship. But they didn't and optimism beat pessimism.

It was like that in the hospital in 2022.

We could understand the severity of Murdo's condition. We knew we were being told there was nothing more that could be done to prevent him slipping away from us. We just felt instinctively that he wasn't finished with life.

Twelve years earlier, when he had a valve inserted in his heart, a less severe toll had been taken on his body. And it was a much younger man who was combatting complications.

Murdo was unconscious for only five days at that time. When the valve was replaced twelve years later, and complications arose, it meant eight weeks on a ventilator and all of the circulatory problems that entailed.

His operation had taken place on 9 September and Murdo came round the following week.

On 20 September he went into shock and his blood pressure suddenly dropped. It was four days before his sixty-fourth birthday.

I used to call the hospital at five o'clock in the morning every day and pass on to the girls the news of his condition and how the night had gone for Murdo.

They kept a daily chart of his progress, or regression, and it was a stressful time. So much so, I started to faint without warning.

It happened once in Mhairi's car. It happened another time when I was visiting Murdo in hospital with our youngest daughter, Marina, and she had to scream for help because it was late at night and she was on her own with me.

The strain on my heart left the doctors with no option but to hospitalise me for three days, which Murdo knew nothing about because he was asleep and showing no signs of coming round.

Murdo's cardiologist was a man called Professor Colin Berry. He came to see us when his patient was at his lowest ebb and we were living in hope of a positive development.

The professor's suggestion was that we should acknowledge Murdo's birthday by getting as many messages from family members and friends as we could and playing them to him to see if it would spark any form of recognition.

One of our grandchildren, Fergus, is Rhino mark two. He loves his football and he loves his papa.

His message implored Murdo to get out of hospital and get back to having a kick-about with him.

It was all very moving and we played the messages faithfully every day.

But there was one song that meant a lot to Murdo. It's called 'Don't Give Up On Me' and it's sung by a performer called Andy Grammer.

The lyrics just seemed to be so appropriate to the situation we were in and so inspirational and uplifting at the same time. The song is all about fighting for someone and never giving up, even when things seem hopeless. It felt like it could have been written for us.

It makes him cry to this day whenever he hears that song, and all of the girls have it on their mobile phones from the time when they were lifting those devices to his ear in a hospital room.

When those girls set their mind to something then anything is possible.

We went to Germany when Murdo was playing and within three months of arriving in Dortmund, Gilan, Mhairi and Marina were fluent in the language. After six months they had the mannerisms as well as the language. They were, to all intents and purposes, German girls.

The club couldn't understand at first why I didn't want to enrol them in what was basically a school for the children of British Army members serving in Germany. I told them that, if nothing else, I wanted our time abroad to give the girls a second language. Children listen and repeat, so that's why they were fluent almost immediately.

I was self-taught, but I was still fluent enough to actually teach German in a school in Helensburgh by the time Murdo had finished at Borussia Dortmund.

The Bundesliga game I remember best was when Dortmund played Bayern Munich at the time when the legendary Franz Beckenbauer was helping to run the club that had made him the most famous football person in Germany.

I sat near to him during the match and the man they called the Kaiser was more like royalty. People stared at him in awe wherever he went.

But the Rhino doesn't do staring.

When Beckenbauer went into the opposition dressing room at the end of the game, Murdo did what no Dortmund player dared to do. He struck up a conversation with the Kaiser and the two of them got on famously. Murdo's teammates couldn't believe he had been so forward but they hung on his every word when he revealed the details of his chat with the great man.

That was the Murdo we knew and loved and wanted back in our everyday lives in 2022.

We wanted every avenue explored regarding the possibility of a recovery and no assumptions to be made about his time being up. And so, one morning, we went into his hospital room and found Murdo sitting up in bed reading the English translation of Wim Jansen's book about his life in football. It was an incredible moment.

On 13 November they moved him out of the High Dependency Unit and into a ward. By the time he left the hospital to go home, Murdo had spent over one hundred days fighting for his life.

Age had made him more stubborn than ever to succeed.

He fought. And he fought when he was almost down to his last breath.

Even when we were told there was nothing left.

22

Paul Lambert on Murdo

DORTMUND IS AN UNASHAMEDLY working-class area of Germany. The people who support Borussia Dortmund value players who work hard above all others.

Murdo MacLeod is as much of a revered name there today as he was when he played for the side in the 1980s. He was the person who laid down the foundation for me there before I joined the club and had the good fortune to be part of the team who defeated Juventus to win the Champions League final in 1997.

If it hadn't been for the impact Murdo made on German football in general and Dortmund in particular, I would have arrived in the country as Paul Who? But a path had been cleared for me, so the fans knew what they were getting with regard to my style of play.

In Germany the philosophy is that every player has a clearly defined role within the team structure. If everyone carries out their individual responsibilities then the belief is that everything else falls into place naturally.

Murdo refers to himself as being like a thief for the team, stealing the ball from the opposition and giving it to the creative players on his side, and I can relate to that description because I saw myself fulfilling that job description as well.

I think of Murdo and me as having had an inner fire. The gold-dust players I was with, like Karl-Heinz Riedle, Andy Möller and Lars Ricken, needed people like us around about them.

Murdo won the German Cup when he was in Dortmund and whenever I go back there to play in Legends games or attend functions associated with the club, his is always the first name to be talked about. He is a superstar there to this day, I can assure you.

And hard work is still his defining characteristic. It certainly was when he convinced me to leave the Champions League holders and sign for Celtic in November of 1997.

I could have gone anywhere in Europe after Dortmund beat Juventus 3–1 in the final. I had offers from Spain and Italy as well as other clubs in Germany, but Murdo was a persistent caller from Scotland. My answer was always to reject the idea of moving back home because I loved Germany, the club and the fans in Dortmund. Then I went back to Scotland to play in a World Cup qualifying tie for the national team against Belarus.

The game had been switched from Hampden to Pittodrie and I was in the Aberdeen boot-room when I suddenly found myself with unexpected company. I was literally cleaning my boots in preparation for the kick-off when Murdo walked in with Wim Jansen and closed the door behind them. They came straight to the point and said they had come to make one last pitch for me to sign for Celtic and help the club win the league title that would stop Rangers from winning Ten in a Row.

I didn't need to be told anything at all about the significance of that achievement, if it happened, and my personal circumstances had altered at the time because one of my children had become unwell and a move back to Scotland had turned into a welcome idea. I went back to Dortmund and told the club I wanted to join Celtic, and the reaction was overwhelming when the news became public knowledge.

My last ever game for Borussia Dortmund was a Champions League match against Parma, which we won 2–0 at home. I went upstairs to the club offices at midnight to sign the forms that would make me a Celtic player and the secretary and general manager were still pleading with me not to leave. Before then I had been told to take a lap of honour on the pitch because the crowd were refusing to go home until I appeared.

My mind was racing. There were people crying and Dortmund banners being draped over the bonnet of my car outside the stadium. I was questioning my own mind and suffering from an inner turmoil that wouldn't leave me for some time after that, but, in the end, I had given Murdo and Wim my word that I would join them at Celtic Park.

You could hardly call my start in green and white the most auspicious possible. We lost to Rangers and Motherwell in quick succession and my displays were poor in those games and in others. I was still coming to terms with leaving Germany in the highly emotional way I had done, so much so I went to see Wim for a meeting.

It was the night before we played Dundee United in the League Cup final at Ibrox and the team was staying in the Cameron House Hotel on the banks of Loch Lomond. Just before dinner I went to Wim's room and told him what was going through my mind.

I admitted I knew I wasn't playing well and I also told the manager I was convinced in my own mind that I would get back to normal and be the player Celtic thought they had bought.

But, in the meantime, I asked Wim to consider not playing me in the cup final because there were others who deserved to start the match before I did. Players who had taken the club to that cup final and merited the right to be chosen ahead of me.

Wim said he would think about it and, when the team was read out, I wasn't in it. The important thing was that Celtic beat Dundee United, and I then started to make an impact on the pitch.

Murdo talked to me a lot at that time because we had this bond created by having had the same experience of having played in Germany. I could confide in him and he helped me get my game back in gear.

The pivotal moment of that season, for me and the team, was the 2–0 win over Rangers at Celtic Park at the beginning of the New Year. Anyone who remembers that game will recall that I scored Celtic's second goal and then took off for a celebratory run that was, to my way of thinking, the reaction of a man who had just had the weight of the world lifted from his shoulders.

Everyone knows what happened after that. The team embarked on a run which concluded with Celtic beating St Johnstone on the final day of the season to become league champions.

That's a bald statement of fact. I would put what happened another way. I would state that what Wim and Murdo achieved that season was almost miraculous.

We had a team full of good players, but there wasn't great depth to the squad as a whole. If we had been troubled by injury problems in a sizeable way then we would have been in real trouble. Thankfully, that didn't happen and we were able to hold off the strongest Rangers team I had ever known.

Walter Smith had a side of real men and was blessed with exceptional talents like Paul Gascoigne and Brian Laudrup.

We had a managerial combination that had been put together almost on the hoof when Murdo met Wim for the first time at the pre-season training camp.

Their strength lay in the chemistry between them.

Wim had a fantastic career behind him in the game, having won the European Cup and played in a World Cup final for Holland. He came into the treatment room at Celtic Park one day wearing his World Cup final shirt and made a joke about it being a little tight for him. The players there, including myself, had a laugh but I knew there was serious intent behind that moment of light relief. This was a man of real substance in the game.

Wim might have been paired with Murdo in front of a sceptical public to begin with but they were the perfect foil for each other. There was an intensity about that season that you could have reached out and touched. On a personal level, I lapped it up because I thrived on the tension that increased from week to week.

I think of the two men who guided us as the figurehead and the buffer. Wim reminded me of my coach at Borussia Dortmund, Ottmar Hitzfeld. He never lost his temper and flew into a rage because that wouldn't get any of us anywhere.

Wim used to tell me that if I saw something was wrong on the park I was to change it without asking him first. He said he would be angry if I didn't act on my own judgement.

Murdo had been a playing part of great Celtic teams from a young age and he was eternally upbeat about the club. He told us he knew we were going to win the league title that season because we were the best team in the division.

In my opinion, that was the greatest championship win Celtic ever had because there was so much riding on it, and I don't believe Wim and Murdo have ever been given the proper amount of credit they were due for doing what they did.

The pressure on their shoulders was enormous and I would love to have been a fly on the wall when they had their private moments to discuss the progress of that season.

When I heard that Wim had passed away I sent Murdo a text which said, 'Tell me this news isn't true.'

Now it's Murdo who is dealing with health issues of his own, but he'll battle illness in the same way he approached any other form of adversity during his time in the game.

He has that inner fire I was talking about. I thank him for passing it on to me and I know it will sustain him throughout what lies ahead in the future.

23

Gordon Strachan on Murdo

WIM JANSEN HAD MURDO MACLEOD as his right-hand man at Celtic Park. I had Tommy Burns when I was manager of the club. I replaced the iconic figure of Martin O'Neill, idolised by the Celtic supporters and someone you might have described without fear of contradiction as being a hard act to follow.

Murdo was introduced to a man from the Netherlands he'd never met before and asked to join him in stopping Rangers from winning Ten in a Row by lifting the league title with a squad of players that needed strengthening as they went about their business. I know who had the tougher job, and it wasn't me and my much-loved, dearly departed friend, Tommy.

Coincidentally, Wim knew right away he wanted Murdo to be his assistant as they navigated their way through the demands of a season that was unlike any other when it began in 1997.

I knew Tommy as an opponent at club level and a team-mate at international level. My first words to him when I walked into Celtic Park were, 'Do you fancy working with me?'

I was from Edinburgh by birth and had played in the cities of Dundee and Aberdeen during the Scottish phase of my career. Glasgow was literally a culture shock for me and I dare say Wim must have felt the same.

Murdo and Tommy were revered by the Celtic supporters because of what they had done when they were wearing the club's jersey. They had an intimate knowledge of the way the supporters thought about things and that was as invaluable to me as it must have been for Wim.

I thought I had seen it all, from winning a European trophy against Real Madrid with Aberdeen to joining Manchester United and playing under Sir Alex Ferguson at Pittodrie and Old Trafford.

But nothing, and I mean absolutely nothing, had prepared me for what it is like to manage Celtic.

I can state now, with the benefit of hindsight, why Murdo and Wim's achievement in winning the league title was, in the end, a greater accomplishment than anything I did with Tommy beside me at Celtic Park.

Those two people are now immortals where Celtic's history is concerned because they stopped a dream scenario materialising for their club's greatest rivals.

If Rangers had won the championship that season and accumulated Scottish football's first ever Ten in a Row they would have been, possibly forever, superior to Celtic. And that is what fans want to be in that extraordinary rivalry.

They need to feel superior to the team from across the city.

You could ask a fan today what system of play Wim and Murdo favoured that season and they would tell you they weren't one hundred per cent certain. But what they do know, without a shadow of doubt, is that Celtic were superior to Walter Smith's side and that, in the final analysis, is all that matters.

I didn't appreciate all of this stuff when I agreed to become Celtic manager but I had someone beside me who had an encyclopaedic knowledge of the subject.

There was a time when I was asked in a post-match press conference about the fans singing my name for the first time and my reply was to the effect that I wasn't at the club to get my name sung. I was there to win football matches. Tommy waited until I was finished with the press and then took me aside to instruct me that the supporters didn't want to hear their songs of encouragement for the manager were of no consequence to him. On the basis that Tommy seemed to know all of the supporters personally, I took the information on board and never made that mistake again.

Murdo, with his playing background at Celtic, would have been of similar assistance to Wim but, at the time, I didn't think he could be of sufficient help to actually forge a title-winning team.

I was looking in from the outside and all I could see was a Rangers team that was a well-oiled machine. They had the players and the buying power and Celtic, by comparison, looked like a work in progress.

That much was verified when Celtic lost in consecutive matches against Hibs and Dunfermline to start their league campaign.

I would come to know what that felt like.

My Celtic team lost nine goals in successive European and league matches to Artmedia Bratislava and Motherwell.

I took the hit, as Wim did before me, but we needed Murdo and Tommy to guide us through the more eccentric moments that go beyond the bounds of conventional criticism.

In my time, for example, I was going downstairs at Celtic Park to have a very important team meeting with the players when I met a wedding party walking in the opposite direction to one of the function suites inside the ground.

The groom asked me if I would be in a photograph with him and his new wife and I readily agreed, but the lady in question was taking her time in getting organised and her husband told her in no uncertain terms to get a move on.

What I mean by that is that he said to her, 'Hurry up because he's probably going to get sacked in the morning.'

Do you think for one moment Pep Guardiola or Arsène Wenger ever went through anything like that?

The pressures of the job were non-stop, and to a degree that I thought was unfair on any human being. It was a form of madness.

But Tommy got it. And so did Murdo.

I can laugh about it now, but I can also appreciate the kind of mental strength Murdo would have brought to the job of keeping everyone calm and focused while a city was at a state of fever pitch concerning the outcome of a league title race destined to go down to the wire on the final day of the season.

I was scared of Murdo on the pitch when we played against each other. I wasn't physically intimidated by him, but I knew he could be a better player than me on any given day and I had to be able to raise my game whenever I came up against him.

And I had known that from his very first day as a professional footballer because I shared the field with him when he came on as a sub for Dumbarton's reserve side twenty-four hours after signing for the club as a teenager.

I was going through what I think of as my shit period in the game at that time and would eventually be sold on to Aberdeen.

I remember thinking this young kid was remarkably strong on the ball for someone of his age and that would characterise his time at Celtic when Billy McNeill eventually signed him.

People think my Aberdeen team dominated the early part of the 1980s within Scottish football but Celtic had some group of players who could all look after themselves.

The misconception was that Celtic glided all over the park while playing lovely football but there were hardy boys there like Murdo, Tommy, big Roy Aitken and Paul McStay who could play tasty football and do the dirty jobs as well.

Murdo was mentally strong but always likeable. I knew that from sometimes sharing a room with him when we were abroad with the national side. He took a while to break into the Scotland team but there was no shame in that because we were living through a time of outstanding midfield players who were eligible to play for their country. You need a strong mind to withstand the wait and then come in and do a job.

But football does strange things to people. When the whistle blows to start a game you turn into a devil and behave like a lunatic.

And then you go home.

When you're trying to win a title for Celtic you have to understand that you're constantly working against this wall of noise. So far as the supporters are concerned, and this would have been particularly true of Wim and Murdo during their time together in management, it's not about style.

It's about winning.

When Murdo was playing for Celtic it was a time when you would have found them, Aberdeen and Dundee United, title winners in 1983, ranked in the top fifteen of UEFA's top sides in Europe. Winning the title in Scotland was a real achievement because the quality of the opposition was so high.

It was a slightly different story when Celtic had, under Wim and Murdo, to deactivate that well-oiled machine at Ibrox.

How can I put this without exaggerating?

When you're part of the management team at Celtic and your job is to stop Rangers from winning Ten in a Row you have the happiness of a worldwide fan base in the palm of your hand. And the extent to which they will be able to enjoy their lives is down to how well you do your job.

That is the exaggeration-free truth of the matter and that is why Wim and Murdo are now immortalised in the history of the club.

When I was going for my first title at Celtic Park, I felt as if I would be regarded as the worst manager who ever lived if I failed the fans. That's why I can only imagine what was going through Murdo's mind in the early weeks of 1998.

But I do know, without having to imagine anything, why we put ourselves through this form of stressful behaviour. When I was finally confirmed a title-winning manager at Celtic Park after a win over Hearts, I experienced this glow of satisfaction looking at the fans, the players and the back-room staff going into a state of delirium.

In that beautifully mellow moment, and Murdo knows this to be true, you know you've done it for every Celtic supporter who ever shook your hand or smiled at you. The genuine people you could reach out and touch. These were the people you worked for.

Tommy was a lifelong fan and he cared for all of the other Celtic supporters he came into contact with on a daily basis.

He had a smile for everybody.

The last thing he said to me before he died made me laugh, but the precise words are mine to cherish and to keep to myself for personal comfort. I thought to myself that this couldn't be right. But Tommy was unique, and I could look at him after the title win and know he was lost in that warm glow of satisfaction along with me.

The way Murdo and Wim would have felt when they won the biggest title of them all.

24

Archie Macpherson on Murdo

O N THE FIRST TEE at the Crail Golf Club the distractions are many. The ocean on your right lies patiently awaiting the refuse of the sport, offered up by the slices and hooks of golfers parting sorrowfully with their golf balls.

The gulls screech, the rabbits scurry, the wind never ceases blethering to you and, on one particular day, Murdo MacLeod stepped forward to that tee addressing the elements with a chest-thrusting demeanour that seemed as if he might have been about to take a penalty kick against his famous rivals.

On that May day in 2016 he was my guest, and in the other times we played together it was evident that he had a passion for the game which was obviously more than simply a light-hearted diversion in his life. His competitive spirit was such that I can't recall all that many putts he conceded to me. Although a gentleman in every way, he clearly enjoyed winning that day. But then, could I have expected anything else?

That sturdy frame of his was created for competing in any sporting sphere, and blasting the small ball out of sight and sinking a long putt seemed a fair enough substitute for those other days in the past when he would raise his arms in acclaim for his accuracies with the other ball. As he sent that particular drive soaring into the Fife sky it was clear that age had not withered him, nor had he shed the carapace of determination and commitment that was his prime asset on any pitch upon which he trod.

This was Murdo, though, as friend, broadcasting colleague, and accompanied by my other friend and commentating partner, Andy Walker. For me, the golf was secondary in these outings. Above all, I vividly recall the chat, and the reminiscing, and the anecdotes, which only underlined for me how distant myself, and others in the media, could be in the past, from the men who were effectively keeping us in gainful employment.

It was astonishing that I learned so much about them that previously I could only base on conjecture. And all because of this brotherly love of the pursuit of the wee white ball.

Now, 'brotherly love' is hardly a phrase that was overused in the decades I had to opine about football, particularly when referring to Celtic and Rangers. Indeed, from the earliest days in the 1960s when we were still employing film cameras of the kind that Mack Sennett used in his Keystone Cop days, and we could never guarantee that every goal in a game would ever be seen by the viewers – giving rise to conspiracy theories – it was wise to accept the convention of keeping yourself at arm's length from those two clubs, to attain a kind of diplomatic immunity from predictable censure on bias. Climbing the north face of the Eiger in plimsolls would have been an easier task.

On these days, in the various golf clubhouses with Murdo, it was inevitable that we brought up many tales of the past which were closely connected with how the media handled issues then. Media professional life had changed dramatically since he had started in the game. When he had made his debut for Celtic on 4 November 1978 against Motherwell there were no smartphones, no iPads in existence, and, for heaven's sake no Google, which was still a full twenty years ahead and is now the bosom-companion of any working journalist.

And broadcasting then was also in a dramatic stage of development itself. At the beginning of the 1970s you would not have been able to determine that Murdo had blondish hair. Everything in TV sport was in black and white, until we saw football in colour for the first time from the Mexico World Cup in 1970. So, he would be part of the colour innovation, with his unmistakable mop becoming a beacon of unerring total commitment to the cause, which encouraged his own teammate, Tommy Burns, to say of him once, 'I'm just glad he plays on my side!'

So how did we all react in the media to his appearance in a green and white jersey that day? At the start of that season I had interviewed Billy McNeill who admitted he was looking forward to a personal duel with his great rival John Greig, newly established as they were in their managerial roles. And he did mention that he was looking forward to encouraging young Scottish talent. I took that as simply the stock answer any manager would provide at that juncture.

But then when Murdo ran out of the Celtic Park tunnel at the age of twenty-one, only a day after he had signed from Dumbarton, the manager could clearly be seen as a man of his word, and possessing the kind of independent mind that paradoxically would be his eventual undoing in his first spell at the club. But since Murdo was in a losing side 2–1 that day, you could imagine that the Scottish media did not embark on a profound analysis of the McNeill youth project. For other issues were exciting the imagination. After all, this was only a month after the astonishing return of Jock Stein from his forty-four-day exile in Leeds to become Scotland manager.

So, Murdo's signing was hardly likely to seize the imagination of those of us still in thrall to the great former Celtic manager and the soaring expectations for Scottish international football that accompanied that. It was when Murdo began to make his obvious mark that the media took the shades off their eyes, with the public as well beginning to wade in. I recall the first goal he scored for the club at Easter Road – a shot which typically was from well outside the box and would have disfigured the terracing had not the net intervened. With such a goal comes expectations of more to follow, which he provided on uncannily timely occasions. He was catching the eye of those who were beginning see him as an indispensable asset for the immediate future and, more emphatically, and in a not-too-surprising way, he caught the eye of some of those from the Ibrox community.

My postbag around then was customarily filled with viewers' opinions, in the days long before Twitter, and with equally bad spelling, and could be considered a compendium of human misery and animosity. Some, in particular, were taking notice of Murdo who was now earning sterling reports, not just for those strikes at goal, but for an attitude that demonstrated that he was not going to be pushed around on a football field. Quite the opposite in fact. In other words, he showed the bearings of a potential powerhouse for Celtic in midfield, in the tradition of, say, a Bobby Murdoch. This intrigued some of my correspondents, out there in the nooks and crannies of footballing gossip, conspiratorial whisperings and lurid fantasies – especially those obsessed with the one-upmanship in which they perceive Ibrox and Celtic Park to be continually engaged.

Some of them were vehemently critical of the club they supported on the other side of the city by often ending their epistles to me with 'Aye Ready'. Crudely put, their views were based on the 'one of us' notion. How could such a talent, who was brought up 'in the shadow of Ibrox' as one put it and went to school at Douglas Academy in Milngavie, end up at Parkhead? A familiar pattern of thinking that was generationally entrenched.

In another society the fact that a manager signed a player simply because of his abilities would hardly raise an eyebrow. So, if the 'one of us' held fast with certain supporters – although to this day I have no idea where Murdo's sympathies lay before he started shaving – in the minds of those who think that way, clearly seeing him in a green and white jersey was like driving a special stake through their hearts. As he did on one very special evening.

In fact, Murdo was simply representing a healthy Celtic tradition that placed ability above all else. But the fact that such interpretations were being laid on a simple transfer revealed the kind of lurid atmosphere that the media had to contend with.

'Is he one of us?' was a question which underpinned many views on anybody who played, watched, wrote about, or commented on the game.

So, in our chats in much later years, I was in the position to inform both Murdo and Andy what life had been like for the entire media under Stein. The big man had a firm belief that most of the press and broadcasters were sympathetic to the other side of the city. He didn't hide that in the least. His way of approaching what he assumed was a naturally biased media was to turn his back on the avuncular manner of the gentlemanly Jimmy McGrory, and make us all approach him like we were attempting to defuse an unexploded bomb. Respect, nay, constant apprehension followed in the early days of his reign.

That reminiscing of the Stein era to Murdo and Andy was relevant because they were the beneficiaries of that revolution. However imperfect the relationship with the media might have been in Murdo's time at Celtic Park, it was nothing like the trench warfare of the Stein era as he fought and won renewed respect for his club.

Added to that was the salient fact that there was no social media. The Wild West of Twitter, Facebook and umpteen burgeoning websites were still far distant when Murdo ventured forth that day against Motherwell. The Scottish newspapers, 'Scotsport', 'Sportscene', Radio Clyde and BBC Radio Scotland established the public platforms of opinions which could range from adulation to mutilation. But it was all parochial. Murdo and colleagues personally knew their admirers and detractors which could lead to some dramatic confrontations, which I know to my own cost. But, essentially, it was more human and immeasurably healthier compared to the brutish anonymity of assaults which can flood into all our electronic gadgets.

I know that Murdo and his generation look back with a sense of relief that while they were playing they did not encounter the scurrilous nature of such technological advance. He benefitted hugely, though, by being under a manager in Billy McNeill who understood the value of the media and was able to sort out those whom he trusted to be straight with the club. I cannot recall a time when I was refused access to a player. It's not that the manager was naive. He simply blended common sense with a shrewd understanding of the kind of publicity which benefitted the club.

Of course, an important element of the respect which Murdo was accorded throughout the media was simply what he characterised. When I think of the times I commentated on his performances it was as if I was seeing him as the gyroscope of the Celtic side; his upright, thundering performances lending them stability as well as power.

At the time of his signing, I can recollect a guarded reaction amongst my colleagues pondering the value of such a signing. As he was a complete unknown to me, I suppose I also placed him in the category of a McNeill gamble. Doubts, though, in the value of the transfer quickly evaporated.

Although he was increasingly influential in midfield, it was his goals which gave him identity, and led me to hyperventilate sometimes in commentary when he let fly. That is the kind of achievement that lifts a midfielder out of the anonymity of the hard slog.

One goal, of course, stands out like a priceless jewel among the fifty-five he netted for the club. It was on Monday, 21 May 1979. The media build-up to that game against Rangers, who were arriving at Celtic Park on the verge of winning the treble, was affected in two ways.

Firstly, the general feeling amongst my colleagues, and which I honestly shared, was that even at the home of their great rivals, Rangers were likely to prevail, aided by the momentum they had gathered in lifting their two trophies previously and inspired by the huge incentive that comes with the Treble dangling temptingly near.

Secondly, Scotland were to play England at Wembley five days later and I felt that within BBC Scotland there was more emphasis being placed on our production of that event as, traditionally, we regarded a trip to London for that international match as a bigger engagement than any other event on the globe.

Over and above that, what made BBC Scotland tend to downplay the significance of the Parkhead match was that we could not provide television coverage ourselves. The game had been rescheduled for a Monday evening. That sounds simple enough. But although I still retain great admiration for the BBC, in those days it was inflexible – a little like an oil tanker that takes an eternity to turn from one direction to another. Football was not made for Mondays in their planning.

I recall being ridiculed like Oliver Twist for going and asking for more. It was not to be. Our department was enraged. We then learned that STV had stepped in. For us at the BBC, in my friend Arthur Montford's phrase, this was a 'stramash'. And then, to our great shameful, snidey glee, we discovered that the production crew at STV were to go on strike and that the treasured prize had been snatched from their grasp also.

Selfishly, at that time, we hardly considered the fact that one of the most historic games in Scottish football would not be covered by any public service broadcaster. BBC

Scotland could only provide radio commentary and, of course, had their biggest audience in a generation.

And so to that last goal by Murdo that put the game beyond Rangers' reach and was voted the best ever by the Celtic support, and worthy of technicolour in their ten-man 4–2 victory. However, the events are seen now as if shrouded in a grey veil, despite Celtic's own cine-crew valiantly recording the game in that emergency. Importantly, it was recorded for the record but lacks the golden lustre of the occasion.

I talked about that to Murdo once, and since his relation-ship with the supporters was like that of a man speaking of his own family, the regret he expressed about lack of proper television coverage was far from vainglorious, but about how the legions had been denied something that deserved to have been shown live to the entire country. Still, the fact that you can still see Murdo's shadowy shape lifting his arm in tribute to the noise coming from the Jungle, after scoring the fourth goal, cannot fail to be iconic and a symbol of a unique triumph.

It was a free kick that finished me as a commentator with Murdo. By that I mean it was the last words I ever spoke about him on the air. Just before half-time in the Stadio Delle Alpi in Scotland's World Cup game against Brazil on 20 June 1990 on a dull, dampish, un-Italian day, the South Americans were awarded a free kick. Branco, their left-back, stepped forward to take it. His kicks, we were told, could flatten a Pamplona bull.

This one struck Murdo fully on the head. He ended up on the turf, forcing me to use a word I never thought I would associate with him, 'motionless'. He was uncon-scious, recovered, but had to be taken off, and has lost all memory of that match which Scotland were to lose 1–0. He did recover but, buried beneath other news about him with his new club Borussia Dortmund, was the fact that they would send him for brain scans as the result of aftershocks from that incident, even weeks later.

He tells that tale of black-out recovery well. Indeed, in all the times I was in his company I learned he was a great raconteur himself, and he and Andy and I often swapped tales of derring-do that, as a commentator, I had observed merely from the outside. But, inevitably, I had to point out to them how this obsessive suspicion about the sympathies of commentators and journalists was as endurable and as thorny as the Scots thistle. And had to be handled with caution.

Murdo might have kept in mind what I said to him about that when his footballing career came to an end and he was inevitably snapped up by the BBC as a regular pundit. He was the perfect fit for them. Clean-cut, articulate, knowledgeable, he ticked all their boxes. Authoritative views from experience across the continent of Europe, having done the equivalent of a Master's degree at Borussia Dortmund, lent him total credibility in a traditionally hostile Scottish environment.

Then, many years later, came rumours to my ears that sent the shivers up the spine – rumours of an undetermined illness, of a gaunt appearance, then of a protracted near-death illness – leading many of us firstly to incredulity, and then to a bewildering relief on hearing of his gradual and successful fight for survival.

So, in positive rehabilitation and with his instinct for competition aroused, the first tee at Crail Golf Club expectantly awaits his triumphant return. The North Sea will be no kinder, the gulls will still ridicule, the wind will still muscle-in, the putts might not drop on cue, but even the roughest of elements will sound like a triumphal chorus for the man who snatched victory from the jaws of the Grim Reaper.

25

Davie Provan on Murdo

THE 4–2 GAME WAS THE GREATEST NIGHT in Celtic's history after the winning of the European Cup final against Inter Milan in Lisbon in 1967.

Murdo and I knew it was, because we had heard the then-chairman of the club, Desmond White, tell a frenzied home dressing room that was the case after he had appealed for calm long enough to make his emotional address to everyone who was there.

It was the kind of night that only happens to Celtic.

And the aftermath was a bit special as well. I took off into the night with Tommy Burns and Johnny Doyle. Once we had run out of pubs that were still open there was a move to a city-centre casino where the carousing could continue.

And when that option was exhausted Tommy knew of an Italian restaurant run by a pal of his called Rocco, where 'la dolce vita' was enjoyed until five o'clock in the morning.

At that point I went home to Langbank, had a shower and went back up to Celtic Park for a photo shoot with the league championship trophy that was scheduled to start at 10 a.m.

According to club legend, the groundsman had earlier opened the front door to the stadium and found two former players, whose names will be discreetly withheld, fast asleep in the boardroom.

It was that kind of night.

If Celtic had won the European Cup the following season it wouldn't have meant as much, or felt as good, as that victory over Rangers in a game that took on a life of its own.

It was a night demanding of hitting the town with a vengeance.

But there was one player who turned up for the photo shoot bright-eyed and bushy-tailed, with not a celebratory mark on him or the merest suggestion of alcohol on his breath.

Murdo MacLeod.

Murdo was the model professional and the perfect family man, even when the dressing room had a major achievement to celebrate. I lost count of the Saturday nights when he was over the Erskine Bridge and on his way home to Mhairi and their daughters before the rest of us had reached our hostelry of choice for a pint.

Managers love it when their players get married young and settle down to a life of domestic bliss, and Murdo was a textbook example of why domesticity was a good idea.

He was the fittest, strongest and quickest player at Celtic.

I'd known him since we played against each other as part-timers at Dumbarton and Kilmarnock. The last time we did that there were rumours of Murdo going to Aston Villa and I wished him well for the future as we stood in the tunnel before the game started.

But both of us were destined for Celtic, and I like to think we made a difference to the team who would finish the championship with a night that is enshrined in folklore for the Celtic supporters.

We had boundless energy and endless ambition, and we were excited simply by being at a club as big as Celtic.

I could truthfully say I played in better Celtic teams than the one who won that league title, but I was never in a dressing room with greater spirit or togetherness. Dressing rooms are habitually made up of people whose aggressive instincts are such they would, metaphorically speaking, kill their granny in order to win matches. Nobody had that mindset to the degree Murdo possessed it. He was the worst loser I ever met in my life. From the football pitch to the golf course, his refusal to accept defeat was legendary.

He and I also had young legs to bring to a team who had lots of experienced players in it, like Danny McGrain, Andy Lynch and Bobby Lennox.

Scotland had been hit by a particularly severe winter during that season and every team came back off a two-month break to face a backlog of games which sometimes meant playing three times in a week to catch up.

We thrived on that tight schedule, all the way to the night of nights.

The dressing room before kick-off against Rangers was, in terms of the atmosphere, the most highly charged I had ever known. Big Billy was a man-manager without peer and his words to the players were awe-inspiring. His speech was all about the opportunity we had to write our names into Celtic's history on an individual and collective basis. It was the most outstanding and memorable team talk of my entire career.

But when Bobby Russell scored for Rangers to make it 2–2 with minutes of the game remaining, the pages of the history book we wanted to occupy could have been refused us.

And then the fairy-tale aspect attached to Celtic, which was Big Billy's copyright, kicked in. We scored a third and I knew there was hardly any time left when Murdo gathered the ball. I was screaming to him to play it to me so that I could take it for a wander out near the corner flag and kill the time remaining to the final whistle. My screams went unheeded and Murdo unleashed one of his trademark, long-range efforts to settle the game beyond argument.

I just remember falling to my knees and resting my forehead on the grass, shaking with anticipation because I knew the final whistle would signal our championship win.

I didn't bother asking Murdo why he had ignored my tactical advice for fear of the consequences. He tended to know more about these things than me.

Years later, when we were a goal down to Dundee United in the 1985 Scottish Cup final, Celtic had a late free kick. It was agreed beforehand that Murdo would take any of those set pieces if they were outside the penalty box.

On that day, he sized up the situation and then said to me, 'I think you could find the top right-hand corner from here.'

I took the kick, found the designated area of the goal, and we had an equaliser that was followed by a winner from Frank McGarvey.

You didn't argue with Murdo, but Mo Johnston made the mistake of doing so before that final began and sparked the most bizarre pre-match rammy in Hampden's history.

Murdo had a ritual prior to kick-off which involved a soak in the bath followed by a rub-down from Jimmy Steele, our masseur. He was just about to get up on the massage table in the dressing room when wee Mo nipped in ahead of him. Murdo's instruction to Mo was as concise as it was explicit, but the guidelines weren't followed, so he took matters into his own hands. One word led to another and soon there were players jumping in to keep the pair of them apart. And this was ten minutes before kick-off at the national cup final.

You would never have wanted to get involved in a scrap with Murdo because he was so physically strong. Unless you were Jackie McNamara senior, of course.

Jackie was at Hibs and he and Murdo had a coming together at Easter Road. They were about to lock horns like stags before the salvage corps comprising players of both sides arrived to stop a serious incident. But that was the kind of aggression Murdo possessed on Celtic's behalf, whether he was a player or a coach.

I was part of the commentary team for Radio Clyde at Celtic Park on the day Murdo and Wim Jansen stopped Rangers from winning Ten in a Row. There were people all around me who were paralysed with fear at the thought of what it would be like if Celtic failed to beat St Johnstone. When Henrik Larsson scored his early goal to put Celtic ahead, I assumed they would go on and score four or five, but paralysis wasn't confined to the seated areas that day. Especially when St Johnstone could, and should, have levelled the scoring. Harald Brattbakk's late winner regulated everyone's breathing, but I didn't detect a smidgin of doubt over the outcome whenever I looked at Murdo down on the track.

He has had the most remarkable career, ticked every box and has a CV others can only dream about.

And he was over the Erskine Bridge and home for a quiet night in before the revellers among us had finished their first pint.

26

Sanjeev Kohli on Murdo

I FIRST MET MURDO MACLEOD when I was guest of honour at the St Andrew's Sporting Club and he had been invited there to watch the boxing with friends who were members. It was, remarkably, only a matter of weeks before he would suffer the medical trauma which almost cost him his life.

He came over to speak to me and tell me how much he and his family enjoyed *Still Game*, the television programme for which I am probably best known because of my character, the shopkeeper, Navid Harrid.

My immediate reaction was to think that I should have been the one to go in the opposite direction and introduce myself to Murdo, who had been a big part of my interest in football from an early age, and tell him how much I admired him as an entertainer.

Not the other way round.

My family came to Britain from India and I was born in London, but we moved to Glasgow when I was just three years old. I have this vague, pre-school recollection of watching football on 'Sportscene' in our new home in Bishopbriggs. I had no allegiance to any team because I was Asian and we were immigrants with no background in football, but all of that changed as I grew older. I was sent to St Aloysius College, a Catholic school where Celtic was the team of choice for the vast majority of the pupils.

Murdo was an influential part of the team I first started to watch, and I thought he controlled the middle of the park for Celtic.

I have to admit my favourite player in the side was Charlie Nicholas. I thought he could do things no other player in Scotland was capable of doing. Charlie simply had star quality from the outset. Then there was a genuinely world-class player in the side like Danny McGrain as well. Murdo was box-to-box on the park, and I loved that, as much as I was thrilled by the players who succeeded him in that role at Celtic, like Stan Petrov.

We were supposed to play rugby at St Aloysius and I actually hated the game. It was football in general, and Celtic in particular, for me.

I have always been in awe of players like Murdo and when I met him it was nice to discover he was engaging and had a friendly disposition. We kept in touch and he invited me to what's known as the Sky Box at Celtic Park, a corporate hospitality facility where I could watch the games with my son, Vinay.

I was always taken by the way Celtic embraced this belief that people came to their ground to be entertained by the team after they had paid their hard-earned money to take a seat. It's the kind of philosophy that's also part of my world, whether it's a theatre audience we're talking about or the people who sit down in their living rooms to watch a television programme like *Still Game*.

There's a working-class philosophy attached to all of it so far as football is concerned. I am the son of an immigrant and I float through the class system as someone who went to a fee-paying school but was irked by the thought that I should think of rugby as somehow being better than football.

I still play football several times a week and I'd be better at it than I am if I had been allowed to develop my skills in school time. That's why I'm in thrall of players, present or past, like Murdo. I think it's almost surreal when they think of me as a friend.

I always kept in touch with Murdo and his wife, Mhairi, and found their family to be made up of such terrific people. When I was told he had come off the ventilator that had been keeping him alive in hospital I decided I had to go and see him in person rather than send my best wishes on the internet. My visit happened to coincide with the day of his daughter's graduation ceremony and the room gradually filled up with family and friends. It led to an impromptu celebration with me and the MacLeods re-enacting some of their favourite scenes from *Still Game*!

I remember, when he was at Celtic, always called me Navid, and not Sanjeev, whenever we met. That's not a problem for me. Navid is the character that I'm most associated with and if they dress me up in his outfit and bury me in it then I'll have no complaint when that day comes. I would only see it as a compliment.

Murdo is best known for having played for Celtic after all and there are parallels between the life of a footballer and that of an actor and writer. We have led aspirational lives. Murdo only ever wanted to play football for a living and although I was a relative latecomer to the entertainment industry at the age of twenty-four, I was of a similar frame of mind when it came to having tunnel vision.

Asian families tend to be aspirational. The parents firmly believe their children must aspire to do better than them, which is why they hope they will turn out to be doctors or lawyers.

I happen to think my son shows signs of being a promising footballer and I like going to watch him play, as Murdo's dad did when he was growing up in Milngavie.

Football was the thing that made Murdo happiest in life, and if that is true of my son then I can only see that as a good thing. I want him to enjoy his life. I want him to wake up every morning and be glad he's going to do what he enjoys most of all. If that means becoming a professional footballer then I can only hope he goes on to be anything like as successful as Murdo was at Celtic, Borussia Dortmund and Hibs.

Football is such a precarious business, particularly when the end of your playing days is in sight. Time is a cruel mistress. I could put on a stone in weight and get older, but that wouldn't affect me as a writer or performer. I would have a longer career span.

Football is different.

That's why I admired Murdo's move into coaching and management and the success he made of that time in his life after he had stopped playing the game.

His role in life now is to restore his health to a higher standard after surviving what could have been a terminal illness. If life can be cruel, sometimes it must be doubly hard to be struck down by medical trauma when you were previously a superbly fit athlete.

I love to hear Murdo tell his stories of the time he had at the highest level of the game, and I look forward to hearing many more. He has known adulation in his time and now he needs concentration for the job of entering the next phase of his life.

27

Reflections

W HEN PEOPLE YOU LOVE, respect and admire write such nice things about you, it's very moving. I wanted to include those words from Mhairi, Paul, Gordon, Davie and Sanjeev as well as Pat McGinlay and Wim Jansen Jnr because they offer some different perspectives on Murdo MacLeod. It's not always easy to see ourselves as others see us, particularly when it's during tough times in our life, but it's hard to put into words just how much their contributions to this book mean to me as I reflect on my life, past and future, funny and sad.

There's so much I've enjoyed about my life. I loved my time on the after-dinner speaking circuit, telling stories about my rise from the teenage days as a Dumbarton player to winning everything with Celtic and then going abroad to have three memorable years with Borussia Dortmund.

Not forgetting the acquisition of twenty Scotland caps and the infamous game against Brazil that's best remembered for the fact that I don't remember what happened after being knocked out cold by a free kick.

Going back out to speak to people in that kind of setting is something I have an ambition to do once again, when my recovery from illness is complete. But what I won't do is try to turn the long time I was dangerously ill into a comedy routine.

There are a variety of reasons for taking that stance, chief among them being the fact I don't think treading a fine line between life and death for as long as I did, and the extent of the pain and suffering that was endured by my wife and children as a result, offers an outlet for humour.

Too many people worked too hard within the National Health Service to prevent me from dying for me to turn their efforts into a string of anecdotes for the entertainment of an audience who've maybe come for a night out to get away from problems they might have on their mind.

There is one other, and very good, reason why I would never attempt to make light of what was a grave situation. If anyone asks me about the intimate details of the weeks I spent on a ventilator being kept alive, I have to be very honest and tell them I don't have a clue. I don't even remember opening my eyes for the first time and starting to breathe for myself.

I have this vague recollection of two workmen climbing a pole outside of my hospital window, but I still don't know if that was actually happening or if I imagined it. I do remember at one point getting a glimpse of the Campsies from my bed in the hospital and thinking how beautiful the hills looked. You would need to ask my wife and daughters about anything else that was going on at that time, however, because I was unconscious.

I get eyewitness accounts of the most important bits, and none was more pivotal than what my sister-in-law, Linda, had to say to the doctor who was basically informing the family that my chances of survival were looking non-existent.

Linda's background was in nursing, so she was used to absorbing information of that description and processing all of it calmly before giving a considered response.

I'm told she simply said to the specialist that there could be no acceptance of my life being at an end and that the family wanted all attempts to be made to give me a fighting chance of survival. That was the life-or-death moment in summary and, as a result, I am now enjoying the days I might never have been spared to see.

How would you make stuff like that sound humorous? There's not a gag with a punchline which can be worked into that kind of storyline.

Another reason why I wouldn't even attempt to turn ventilators, dialysis machines, nurses and doctors into the component parts of a comedy routine is that I wouldn't want anybody to think I was looking for sympathy in the midst of near tragedy. The overt kindnesses I receive and the acts of support I get every day of my life now mean everything to me. I don't need sympathy because I have so many people rooting for me.

The number of men and women who stop to talk and say they are offering up prayers for my full recovery is amazing and I respectfully thank them for thinking of me in that way.

There was one old golf partner I met who told me he was another of the prayer-sayers and then added, 'You used to be such a hard bastard!' I trust the Almighty turned a deaf ear to that bit!

Our next-door neighbours in Dortmund still keep in touch and they go to church every day to pray for me.

How could I not be touched by that kind of emotional, and spiritual, support?

And it's everywhere I go.

Dumbarton's ground is the nearest one to my home and they are the club that started my professional career. Celtic Park is where the story took a dramatic turn for me as player and coach. I go to both grounds to watch matches because they represent the bookends of my career, but I don't visit them to be a figure of pity.

Getting up the stairs from the boardroom area at Celtic Park to the main stand is an exacting business with walking sticks, but every time I make the summit it feels like another step along the way to recovery. And people recognise what I'm doing and make sure they give me the room to negotiate the journey under my own steam.

Nobody walks past me because they can get to their seat quicker than I can manage, and I am not troubled by ego to the extent that I don't want people to see me painstakingly negotiate the journey with the aid of walking sticks.

I used to be out on the park, scoring goals and winning trophies, but I am now what I am, and that is a man who has been desperately ill and is training hard like I used to do as a player in order to get better.

I'm working to look after myself and to stand on my own two feet.

There's no inclination towards feeling life has played a cruel trick on me. I got everything I wanted out of life, and the only thing I truly wanted was to be the best footballer I possibly could be at the highest level of the game.

I have absolutely no doubt there are people who are worse off than me and all I want to do is get better all the time. You get on with life and whatever it has thrown at you because the alternative is not to be here at all, and that was never going to be acceptable for me.

They say everything happens for a reason and I can go along with that way of thinking, even though I couldn't actually give you a reason for what happened in my case. What I can tell you is that every day I try to walk better than I did the day before, and with each passing day I walk with an even bigger smile on my face. I was too well looked after by too many people to feel any other way but determined to pay everyone back for what they did for me.

I have been spared to watch my grandsons play football and aspire to be what their papa was in his time. If I can't get a seat to watch their matches then I go to the car and make sure it has a good view of the pitch. There are people at those games who have no idea who I am because they are too young to remember, but that doesn't matter. I know within myself that I had a career to savour and that's enough.

That career began on 2 November 1978, a life-changing day for me. I didn't think in those deep and meaningful terms at that time because I was only twenty years old and I never really looked too far beyond my next game of football.

But, decades later, I still have regular evidence to support the theory that signing for Celtic on that date would change my world forever.

I am reminded of that being the case whenever I am invited to go, for example, to Texas for a Celtic supporters' convention or to visit Australia at the request of the fans because I am still remembered for what I achieved at Celtic Park decades ago.

Just going to the ground for signing talks with Billy McNeill, Celtic's manager, was my reward for dedicating my life to football from an early age and forgoing all of the other unhelpful distractions that might have got in the way of my ambition to succeed in the game at the highest level.

Scoring the long-range goal against Rangers that won the league title at the end of my first season at Celtic, or the one I hit from distance at Ibrox to end the classic 4–4 draw in the derby there didn't just happen by accident. I disciplined myself from the age of ten to strike the ball from distance.

We had a pitch attached to my primary school in Milngavie and I would stand on the halfway line and repeat, over and over again, the act of hitting the goal from that far out. I would do it during school hours and, when the building was shut, I would climb over the fence and repeat the exercise until I had mastered my technique.

The school building was only fifty yards from my family home and it became my private place to learn my trade. You could call it tunnel vision or whatever else you like, but I had an adolescent's view of what I wanted my adult life to look like and I would pursue my aim to the exclusion of all else.

That's why the sign that said 'No Ball Games' on the grass park opposite my house might as well have been written in a foreign language for all the attention I paid to it.

Playing football was my obsession.

There was a physical education instructor at Douglas Academy in Milngavie by the name of Davie Hannah, who carried himself with military bearing and could see the seriousness of my intentions straight away when I started there. He helped push me to the limits of human endurance on a daily basis and was dismissive of others who weren't as committed as me.

'Ham and eggers,' he would call them and focus on the boy who was desperate to get on.

Davie's long-term plan was that I should take the talent he would help hone to Rangers and sign for them. He was gutted when I signed for Dumbarton while I was still at school, and told me as much. I don't know what he would have thought on 3 November 1978 when he read that I had then moved on to Celtic.

I didn't think about money when I was of school age, of course, but I had to think about it years later when I sat down with the legend that was Big Billy to talk terms over my move from Dumbarton. I had never actually met Billy in person before that day. Television appearances and newspaper photographs were all I had ever seen of him.

And suddenly there he was, sitting down at the opposite end of a desk and looking like a film star to me.

I didn't even have an agent to negotiate on my behalf. I only knew of the existence of one players' representative in Scotland at that time, a man called Bill McMurdo, but I was of a mind to be a big boy and act on my own behalf. It was the way I had dealt with everything in my life up until then.

I had a firm understanding of my worth and that was to be used as a bargaining tool. I might have been young but I had played over one hundred first-team games for Dumbarton and I was a player who brought goals to his team. Or the one he would be joining if the talks went well.

At the same time, I was deeply conscious of the fact I was speaking to a bona fide icon at the club and so, when the time came to accept the first offer that was put in front of me or do my best to argue like an experienced negotiator for a substantially better deal, I did what any self-respecting twenty-year-old would do.

I accepted the first offer.

And I can tell you in all honesty that I left the ground that day as a £100,000 signing who had agreed to a weekly wage that was less than I was earning as a Dumbarton player.

I remember the sum of money involved right down to the last penny.

I joined Celtic on a weekly wage of £114.30.

The reason why I was getting more money where I had been before was quite simple. I was a part-time player at Dumbarton and supplemented my earnings there by working in a local whisky bond by day. But now I was joining a world-renowned football club and didn't have to do anything other than play football for a living.

I felt like a millionaire.

My first weekly wage at Celtic Park was the sum of money one of today's players might leave on the dinner table as a tip after he's had a nice night out with friends at a restaurant. But I will never look back on those days and wish I had been born into another, more lucrative time for football players.

I didn't envy the Portuguese player at Celtic, Jota, when he left the club as part of a £25,000,000 transfer to the Gulf states, and for a wage that was truly astronomical and genuinely life altering.

The medical problems that subsequently affected my daily life after I'd retired from football don't cause me to look back and wish I had enjoyed myself any more than I did when I was young and carefree.

I got out of the game, financially and in every other way, all that I ever wanted, and I have no complaints whatsoever.

All I ever wanted when I was growing up was to be a footballer, and to make that dream come true at a club like Celtic fulfilled me. No retrospective regrets. No hang-ups with the benefit of hindsight.

When I was a kid in the 1960s, there were few cars that ever came down our street. I learned my good habits with a ball by practising outside my parents' house on a morning, noon and night basis. I put my heart and soul into preparing myself for a life in football and the game repaid me with a lifetime's worth of memories.

We're even.

To be befriended by someone like Billy McNeill to begin with was a sizeable reward on its own. He was Celtic. Billy personified everything the club was about, on and off the park, and the gaffer was never anything other than positive and encouraging when it came to furthering my development as a player.

There was more than an element of mischief about him as well. Billy was Celtic through and through and therefore he understood there was nothing more satisfying for our supporters than a win over Rangers at Ibrox.

The new Ibrox, with its four stands and no more terracing, was taking shape when Tom McAdam and I scored the goals that won the game for Celtic there soon after I arrived at the club. Billy was ecstatic in the away dressing room afterwards and hatched a plan which, even though I worshipped the man, I just couldn't go through with under any circumstances.

'C'mon, wee man,' he said to me with a glint in his eye. 'Let's you and I go up the marble staircase to tell Deedle-Doddle what a nice stadium he's got.'

Deedle-Doddle was the nickname the Rangers fans had had for Willie Waddell since he played for the club he would later manage. He also masterminded the reconstruction of the ground once he had joined Rangers' board of directors. But there was no way I was going up the stairs to be an impudent upstart in the aftermath of a win, no matter how delighted I was to be part of the triumphant team.

Billy always made me feel ten feet tall, but I wanted to be that size in our dressing room that day and nowhere else.

And what a dressing room it was at that time. I hear and read a lot today about players going into Celtic Park and Ibrox from abroad and how they need time to adapt to the culture and the football. We had one foreign player at Celtic when I joined the club, Johannes Edvaldsson, and it was the Icelander who christened me the Rhino one day in training. The nickname stuck with the fans for years after that.

Big Shuggie, as he was known, had no difficulty immersing himself in the culture at Celtic Park. And it suited me down to the ground as well.

Billy McNeill was one of that school of managers who subscribed to the belief that young players were better off married with children because it would settle them down on a domestic level and help them avoid the pitfalls that could occasionally arise as a result of being young and fancy free.

I had been married in my teens and started a family before I got to Celtic. There wasn't even any inclination on my part to take my signing-on fee and go on any mad spending spree before my wife, Mhairi, could find out about it. A lager shandy on a night out with the boys in the team was just about the definition of the high life for me in those days.

I was even driving about in a sponsored car, one given to all the members of the first team squad by a businessman called Ian Skelly, and mine happened to be the only one that was green in colour. Tommy Burns begged me to swap with him but, as much as I adored him, I was having none of it.

Nothing troubled me, not even when Big Billy told me I was going with the under-18 side as an over-age player to take part in a pre-season tournament. This was weeks after I had scored one of the goals that won the league title in a match that had instantly become part of the club's folklore. But I didn't protest or throw any toys out of the pram. There were no accusations about my dignity having been injured. No offence taken.

I looked upon Billy as being almost a parental figure where I was concerned, so if that was what he thought was best for me I wasn't about to start an argument. I went to the Netherlands willingly and I scored two goals when we won the tournament's final.

The princely sum of £114.30 per week, a sponsored car, a home of my own and a team that was a joy to play with.

I was living the dream, mate, as a future Celtic manager would have put it.

Epilogue

IT WAS A BIT LIKE BEING BACK in the playing days for me when I made my appearance at a special event for Celtic supporters in Glasgow's Armadillo on 12 May 2023. The occasion was to mark the twenty-fifth anniversary of the club stopping Rangers from winning Ten in a Row by bringing the league title to Celtic Park instead.

I was told beforehand that I was coming on in the second half of the show and there was that old, familiar nervousness as I waited in the wings until my name was shouted out.

I had decided to go public in a newspaper article beforehand which revealed the full extent to which my body had been affected by the aftermath of a heart operation which had developed life-altering complications. I told the truth about no longer having any toes because I wanted to be honest and open, as well as prepare people in the audience that night for the difficulties I was experiencing while trying to walk.

My vow made in print was that I would go on to the stage at the Armadillo unaided and stand on my own two feet while I spoke to the fans. I did it as I promised and I felt grateful for being able to do so, and so did the family I had all around me to share what was an emotional experience.

I wept at regular intervals throughout the night, as I knew I would and my family had assured me I would do, but there was nothing wrong with that.

The whole evening felt like being reunited with my best pals as well as the family of Wim Jansen, the Celtic manager who had stopped Rangers creating history within Scottish football and who had ultimately passed away after living with dementia.

Wim's wife, son, daughter and partners, along with his grandchildren, had made the journey to Glasgow from their home in Rotterdam and that made the night all the more special for me.

To hear the crowd made up of hundreds of Celtic supporters singing 'There's only one Wim Jansen' was a moving experience for all of us, family, close friends and former players alike.

The best way to sum up the emotional impact the occasion had on me is to say that it is profoundly touching to know what you meant to so many people, and I include the ones who were there in the audience who clearly had not even been born yet when Celtic beat St Johnstone at home that day when the league was won in the final fixture of the season.

Chris Sutton, a serial title winner in the days when he was a Celtic striker in Martin O'Neill's side, was the man who was interviewing me on stage. Sutty can be an arch wind-up merchant in print, radio or television, but I knew he was being gentle with me out of respect for my physical condition and I was appreciative of that approach.

As I walked towards him when Wim Jansen jnr had finished talking about me and my friendship with his father, the crowd erupted spontaneously into a chorus of 'Ten Men Won the League'.

That song had been added to the fans' repertoire in 1979 when I scored the final goal in the 4–2 victory over Rangers that came after we had lost the late Johnny Doyle to a sending off.

Since that famous night had been forty-four years earlier, I knew there were literally hundreds of people in the audience who had yet to be born when that memorable match had been played.

But the song and the stories of that night had obviously been passed down from generation to generation and that was the start of the crying game for me.

We had songs to sing and stories to tell and as best I could I told the audience of how it had been when we had to play a friendly match in Portugal after stopping Ten in a Row in 1998. The players were reluctant to go ahead with the match after it had been admitted that Wim was triggering a release clause in his contract and leaving Celtic Park.

He told the players they would indeed be going ahead with the game and told them to stand up, which prompted a team rendition of 'Stand up for the Champions'.

At that moment, every person in the Armadillo stood up and belted out that song with the enthusiasm it deserves.

And I was off again.

It was a night of shared sorrow and tears, as well as unadulterated joy and laughter as the stories were told by the players themselves about a season that was unlike any other.

Simon Donnelly was the one who thought he'd get a special mention in history on the penultimate day of the league season. Sid, as everyone knew him in the dressing room, scored the opening goal of the game away to Dunfermline which came twenty-four hours after Rangers had lost at home to Kilmarnock in the match which opened the door to a title win.

But Dunfermline equalised and the rest is history.

It was the journey to Dunfermline on the team bus which gave Sid the chance to deliver an anecdote which, can I warn you in advance, requires a broad mind and will not be for the easily offended. But it happened and is therefore a matter of public record.

The journey to Fife was made by a lot of people in a state of high excitement that day and the bus carrying the team was hardly going to go unrecognised under those circumstances.

Sid's story concerned the bus taking a turning off the motorway just beyond Cumbernauld.

At that point, and I am trying to put this as delicately as possible in the interests of sensitivity and propriety, a young woman in a car parked by the side of the road removed the top half of her clothing and exposed herself to a coach-load of football players on the way to their work.

To this day I have no idea whether it was supposed to be a bizarre way of inspiring the team or simply a tribute to all of us for the job we had done in getting so close to the winning of a league championship.

Wim kept saying to me, 'Murdo, what's happening?'

I kept telling him I'd explain it all to him later on.

Whatever the young woman's motivation, it temporarily broke the tension that was being felt on the team bus. Not enough to win us the game but still seared on Sid's mind a quarter of a century later.

The night went on in that affectionate fashion and I could sense inwardly that I was having a great time after what had been such a hard time for me. Life had thrown quite a lot in my direction but the warmth I got back from the players and the fans was of immense satisfaction.

People were coming up to me after the formal part of the evening was over and every one of them had the same sentiment to express.

'Murdo, all the best for the future,' was the message I kept hearing, over and over again. It brought everything back to me about the time I had spent at Celtic as a player and a coach.

It also reminded me of the people I had worked with at the club over the decades and how it was to be part of something that is so unique within the game.

The night will never leave my mind because it was as good as any I had ever known and, after all I have been through since my time in football stopped, my first reaction was to be thankful to still be here to have the memory.

It was emotional to say goodbye to the Jansen family when it was all over, but one day I'll go to Rotterdam to meet them again.

It was heartwarming to be back in the company of so many great players who had worked so hard for Wim and me. No awkward personalities. No weird behaviour. Top-class people on a personal level who still revelled in each other's company as if there had been no passing of time since they last saw each other.

The whole event gave me a massive lift with regard to facing a future that the people in the audience had wished me well in negotiating.

I didn't want the day to end, but it did in the early hours of the following morning. I had stood up for so long and been kindly asked to be in so many photographs that my surgically altered feet were in absolute agony.

But I walked on to the stage without assistance and I stood on my own two feet to speak, as I had sworn to do, and that's the way I'll face whatever lies ahead.

Standing up for myself.

Acknowledgements

M Y MEDICAL HISTORY IN recent years demands that I begin by acknowledging the quality of the hospital treatment I have received, along with the care and attention shown to me, at the hands of NHS Scotland. You have my deepest gratitude and thanks.

I also want to thank Black & White Publishing for providing me with the platform to tell my story and my friend, Hugh Keevins, for guiding me through the process.

And I can't speak highly enough of those who have made their contribution to the storytelling, Wim Jansen jnr, Gordon Strachan, Roy Aitken, Paul Lambert, Pat McGinlay, Davie Provan, Sanjeev Kohli and Archie Macpherson.

The fans of the clubs I have played for throughout my career at Dumbarton, Dortmund, Hibs and Partick Thistle have always been important to me and I keep a place for them in my heart.

But the title of this book is the chant the Celtic supporters had for me during the games I played over that tumultuous period in my life. They are forever in my thoughts and I want them to know how much they mean to me and my family.

MURDO MACLEOD

MURDO!
MURDO!

MURDO! MURDO!

From the 4–2 Game to Stopping the Ten

My Autobiography

MURDO MACLEOD

with Hugh Keevins

Black&White

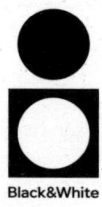

Black&White

First published in the UK in 2024 by
Black & White Publishing Ltd
Nautical House, 104 Commercial Street, Edinburgh, EH6 6NF

A division of Bonnier Books UK
4th Floor, Victoria House, Bloomsbury Square, London, WC1B 4DA
Owned by Bonnier Books
Sveavägen 56, Stockholm, Sweden

All images in the picture section courtesy of the *Daily Record*, except those
listed below, which are courtesy of the author: page 3 (bottom two),
page 4 (bottom), pages 5 and 6 (all).

The publisher has made every reasonable effort to contact copyright
holders of images and other material used in this book.
Any errors are inadvertent and anyone who for any
reason has not been contacted is invited to write to
the publisher so that a full acknowledgement can be
made in subsequent editions of this work.

A CIP catalogue record for this book is available from the British Library.

ISBN: 978 1 78530 713 3

1 3 5 7 9 10 8 6 4 2

Typeset by Data Connection
Printed and bound in Great Britain by Clays Ltd, Elcograf S.p.A.

www.blackandwhitepublishing.com